THE ULTIMATE
Chocolate Book

BY ROBERT LAMBERT
PHOTOGRAPHY BY PATRICIA BRABANT

MITCHELL BEAZLEY

First published in Great Britain in 1990

This edition published in 1993 by Mitchell Beazley
an imprint of Reed Consumer Books Limited
Michelin House, 81 Fulham Road, London SW3 6RB
and Auckland, Melbourne, Singapore and Toronto

Copyright © 1988 Robert Lambert

ISBN 1 85732 282 7

A CIP catalogue record for this book is available from
the British Library

Produced by Mandarin Offset
Printed in China

Contents

Introduction

Desserts hold a curious place in the synthesis of world cuisines. In Asia and Africa especially, cooks often mix sweet with sour, salty and bitter throughout a meal and integrate the craving for sugar. We, however, grow up hearing 'Not until you've finished your dinner...' and learn to earn the sweet by sweating first for our daily bread. Indeed, dessert is often our metaphor for the best of life's pleasures, from the cherry on top to the icing on the cake. My complaint against desserts is that, while they often look good with their squiggly icing and fluffy meringue, they rarely taste as good as they look. ● My own rigorous standard of comparison is based on a farm background – a mother who is an accomplished baker and a grandmother whose cooking career began in northern Wisconsin logging camps at 15. I grew up with wild raspberry jam filled biscuits and eight kinds of sweet rolls. After that it was all a disappointment until I went to Europe. French pastries with their secrets of flavour and texture made an impression that far outlasted memories of the great art I'd gone to explore. ● After five years as an artist and designer in Los Angeles I moved to the San Geronimo Valley near San Francisco – to a stream, redwoods and a large garden. There I began to cook, and, as I looked around, it seemed everyone else had too! The Bay Area food revolution was being born. By the time I got to staging elaborate sit-down dinners for guests I hardly knew, I found I had the palate and desire to join the fray myself. As a child I had spent hundreds of happy hours drawing and building architectural fantasies, so the structural nature of pastry in particular appealed to the latent architect in me. I also wanted to achieve the quality of dessert I knew existed but rarely encountered. ● No one endorses wolfing large portions of rich dessert after every meal, but a small, well-flavoured indulgence savoured is intrinsic to our celebrations. Yet in spite of this there are few notable exceptions to a lack of innovation in the field compared with the exciting achievements in the rest of contemporary food. Besides a lack of examples to draw upon in our favourite exotic cuisines, another reason for this lack may simply lie in the intrinsic differences between dessert and savoury cookery. There is far more chemistry involved; to be a good pastry chef is to be a slave to the secret habits of chocolate, butter, eggs and cream. It's understandable, then, that most pastry chefs are classically trained professionals – and that they become slaves to their techniques and recipes as well, losing their chance for creative freedom. I found the redeeming feature of most dessert components to be that, while volatile in preparation, they are often far more stable at serving time than other foods and more plastic in their range of shapes and forms. Because of this, its heritage of indulgence and its position in the meal as grand finale, dessert provides the opportunity to amaze. ● The architect, graphic artist and cook in me conspired to create a place for myself in the world of pastry. Once asked by a wealthy matron client what cooking school I attended, I hastily replied 'L'Ecole aux Frappes Dures', my high school French for an approximation of 'The School of Hard Knocks', to which she responded, 'Oh yes, that's in Montreal, isn't it'? I sometimes think of myself as one of the great frauds of the San Francisco food world. Not only have I never had the merest shred of formal training, I rarely even use cookery books. ● At the first pastry job I talked myself into I was left to an occasional scribbled note and to my own devices. Between reading, phone calls to Mom, memories of France and help from colleagues I honed a solid repertoire based on my nightly successes in the dining room. I interchanged the component recipes which made up my desserts to expand my range beyond the limits of my education while I broadened my knowledge, eventually compiling a complete kit of versatile recipes. ● Since I knew what I'd learned only from experience rather than what I'd been told, I demystified unnecessarily complex procedures and was able to allow my creative side to explore the possibilities of the various recipes I had mastered. The plate became my stage. I began to work with caterers who produce special events, which is more a branch of show business than any other form of food service.

● Most recently I have developed a market for speciality wedding cakes and edible constructions as centre pieces for special events. In one case I made a four-foot model of San Diego's ersatz Old Globe Theatre from 37 dacquoise cakes, which were assembled on a stage before 300 guests as 37 waiters carried in the pieces on silver trays... What should be of interest to the reader in all of this is that my success is based on so little – and that most of it is right here in this book. ● These intensely flavoured, richly textured basic recipes are based on historical precedent, but I've made them easy and reliable. They are the building blocks I use to create an endless variety of stunning new presentations that keep my clients coming back for more. The ideas presented here will have you surpassing the flair of the finest chefs in the profession. Besides the perfect custard or chocolate sauce, your guests will always remember that shard of marbled chocolate or the new experience of eating with a chocolate-dipped spoon – and link that memory inextricably with you, the host who provided it. What I am presenting here is a full spectrum of the elements in my most successful work, and a portfolio of ways they can be combined to create a new style of dessert that deserves all the fantasies, anticipation, child-like wonder and fun that the idea of dessert can conjure. ● Since it is without doubt the most universally irresistible dessert ingredient, chocolate is the theme I have chosen. This unique, impossible-to-duplicate, natural product contains more than 100 chemical compounds, becomes edible only after a long, complex process that includes fermentation, yet contains no alcohol and bears little resemblance to the seed of the rain-forest tree from which it comes. That chocolate is the only food to melt at exactly the temperature of the human mouth is only one of its secrets. Studies have shown that compounds found in chocolate stimulate the brain in a way that duplicates the state of being in love. The desserts in this book can whip up and quell all kinds of passion – and can stimulate the imagination as well.

Using This Book

There are 23 different dessert presentations pictured in this book. Included in accompanying text is an introduction to the origins of each, a list of equipment needed for assembly, a list of the ingredients and component recipes each contains, an explanation of the assembly procedure, plus notes on how to keep them fresh and how many they will serve. Also included are further notes of interest and lists of alternate components to try with the desserts. These component recipes, numbered 1 to 44, are sorted into six categories: cakes, pastries, fillings and icings, sauces, little sweets and extras and accents and garnishes.

The desserts contain from one to as many as seven components, but in those with the most components several are simply additional garnishes in an elaborate display, and are optional. Every effort has been made to scale the amount of each component recipe to the quantity needed for each of the desserts in which it is pictured. However, it's up to you to gauge visually or by measurement its distribution or division into the number of servings you require.

You may choose in some cases to make a full batch when only a portion of one is called for or to double a batch while you're at it for another use. Especially in the case of some sauces or fillings, many of the component recipes are staples that will last for months frozen or simply refrigerated, convenient for quick desserts.

About notes on keeping I realize that notes on the keeping qualities in recipes here indicate a greater longevity for the finished products than is usually recommended. My estimates are based on solid experience – food for literally hundreds of thousands of people has passed my hands and judgement without a single problem. What I cannot emphasize enough to ensure such a clear record is proper storage and lack of contamination.

Generally, hot items, especially those containing eggs and dairy products, should be cooled to room temperature before chilling. Cover foods tightly in clean containers, and never touch them with your fingers, or with spoons or other implements, after cooking or during storage.

Achieving dramatic presentations Although these desserts are pictured in fantasy settings they can transfer to your table with similar effect.

For plated desserts, forget all about that tiny round called the dessert plate. Dessert is an attraction – and demands a venue scaled to its performance. Use standard dinner plates for composed presentations, so as not to crowd the action.

The importance of precision The use of a ruler and scalpel followed me from my experience in graphic design, but it is just as important in culinary design. Take the time to accurately prepare

your construction elements and you will end up saving time and trouble, in an effortless assembly. Also, if your base is precise the free-form elements, such as squiggles of sauce or broken shards of chocolate are more effectively set off.

EQUIPMENT NOTES

Hand tools Most of the hand implements called for here are in any well equipped kitchen, but in some cases a certain type will be better for pastry than others of its kind. Large commercial-size rubber spatulas are best for folding, as they disturb the batter least. A firm 20 cm/8 in metal palette knife is essential, and it pays to get a good one. I often call for a slotted wooden spatula. As for whisks, any looped wire ones will do, and it may sometimes be convenient to have more than one.

Bowls, pans and measuring jugs As a general rule, stainless steel is the preferred substance of both saucepans and bowls in these recipes. It conducts heat well, withstands high temperatures but cools quickly and is non-reactive. Cast iron or aluminium can easily taint delicate custards or acidic fruit sauces. Heavy-walled pans or those with thick bases are important to the success of custards made without a double boiler, which is an implement I detest – never the right size, too narrow or too deep, either sputtering steam round the rim or burning dry. I replace with the appropriate size saucepan of water under a stainless steel bowl.

Small, medium and large saucepans referred to here are 1 litre/1¼ pints, 2 litre/3½ pints and 3 litre/5¼ pints capacities, respectively. Small, medium and large bowl requirements will be easily met by a basic set of stainless steel bowls, except when a small bowl is used for tinting or dipping small amounts of chocolate. Here a set of ramekin dishes will be useful. Heatproof glass is best for measuring jugs, especially if you're working with caramelized sugar.

A 30 x 42 x 2.5 cm/12 x 17 x 1 in Swiss roll tin is called for repeatedly here, not from professional bias but because it's the best tool for the job. Heavy-gauge metal construction distributes heat evenly, will not buckle in the oven and provides a perfect surface on the back of the tin for many other uses. The capacity of the commercial-size tin makes it more versatile than the home-kitchen size.

Baking parchment, called for throughout is the best lining for tins. Substitutions can be made. Greaseproof paper can be used on the backs of Swiss roll tins when using them to make garnishes, such as chocolate tiles or filigree. Instructions for greasing are particular to each recipe and can't be generalized.

Piping bags and nozzles Three standard plastic or cloth piping bags will be enough to complete any of these creations. Since I abhor most conventional applications of piping anyway, I find the tiny tips sold in cake decorating kits almost useless. Try larger sizes for more drama; get some unusual tips, and play with their possible effects. There are cake decorating supply shops in most large cities.

The single most useful piping nozzle I have ever found is the large 5 cm/2 inch wide, flat filling nozzle with one edge toothed and the other smooth. This nozzle alone has saved me so much time and aggravation that I recommend it exclusively for fillings and for most icing jobs. The endless spreading and smoothing that overworks filling textures and tears delicate cakes is history, with this simple device.

For occasions where a plain, fine stream of sauce or chocolate is required, small strong polyethene freezer bags in 1 litre /1¼ pint or 500 ml /16 fl oz sizes make useful piping bags; a corner can be cut to the exact size needed, and the safe closure prevents the contents from spilling backwards out of the bag. They can be disposed of or cleaned and reused.

Kitchen scales Since so many ingredients are measured by weight, scales are an invaluable asset to precise ratios. It is specially useful in measuring nuts and chocolate cut from blocks.

Electric appliances A large electric beater with an attached bowl is an enormous help in any pastry work above the cake mix level, since long periods of beating are sometimes required. These machines allow you to beat while you proceed with other steps.

Food processors have become so ubiquitous in our homes that I regularly refer to them in my instructions. Key uses for pastry that no other machine can match are creaming butter with sugar or rubbing it into flour. When a blender can be substituted, this is specified.

INGREDIENTS NOTES
Chocolate With flavours in the foreground, the success of these desserts lies in the impeccable quality of their ingredients. It is unfortunate, then, that the most commonly accessible forms of sweet dark chocolate are so dismal, containing large quantities of non-cocoa based waxes, oils and stabilizers. I suggest you use good quality chocolate bought at a specialist shop and forgo the myriad permutations of supermarket chocolate bars. Even buying it in blocks as I do should not be impractical for the home cook; since cocoa butter stubbornly resists turning rancid, this chocolate will keep for several years.

Other types of chocolate used here are unsweetened or baker's chocolate; bittersweet, which contains some sugar; plain, which contains a bit more; regular dark chocolate, which is a little sweeter and milk chocolate, which is sweeter yet and contains milk solids. Unsweetened chocolate is not widely available in Britain. It adds a distinctive taste to recipes. If you ever go to the United States or have friends travelling there, I suggest you stock up. Food halls in large department stores sometimes stock unsweetened chocolate. You may also find it in local shops where there is a large American community. Chocolate essence is called for to boost flavour or where graininess would result from use of any other form.

Finally, there is white chocolate. Yes, I know, it's not really chocolate at all from the view of the laboratory. But if it looks like chocolate, melts like chocolate and is always used as chocolate is, I think we can take the giddy leap of placing it in the same category - on the continuum beyond milk chocolate, since it is substantially sweeter. Actually, of the two basic white types, one is at least a bastard cousin. It contains cocoa butter and is slightly translucent with a yellowish cast and a softer texture. It is therefore not always useable. Then the white cake covering stands in. With its palm oil replacing the cocoa butter, it is whiter, more opaque and of a better texture for tinting, spreading and cutting. However, for simple dipping procedures you may wish to use the better flavoured cocoa butter variety. All chocolate should be kept in a dark place, well wrapped, at cool to room temperature.

Other ingredients All cream in these recipes must be double cream. Unsalted butter is

preferred throughout but specified only where nothing else will do. All milk referred to in these recipes is whole milk. Eggs used here are always size 3 so whatever else you vary in the eggs you choose they must at least be of the same size category to ensure proper ratios, or even appropriate final serving sizes. The most important point is freshness – for flavour, for volume when whipped, even for separating eggs, as the yolks of old eggs tend to collapse. Since eggs are essential to the structure of most of our basic construction materials here, pursuit of the best is no idle quest.

Nuts are often considerably cheaper purchased at health food shops. Nuts should be properly stored to prevent them turning rancid. Store pecans, hazelnuts and almonds in airtight containers and refrigerate if you plan to keep them for more than a few weeks. Nuts with higher oil content, such as pistachios and walnuts, should be kept in the freezer. If you buy nuts in small packages, as you need them, make sure they're from a busy shop where the stock is likely to be fresh.

Granulated sugar has been used in the testing of these recipes, although caster sugar can sometimes increase the volume of egg whites.

Two kinds of flour are used in this book: unbleached plain flour and plain 'soft' flour. In every instance the kind to use is specified. Generally, plain is appropriate for

its bulk in biscuits and pastry; soft plain flour is useful for its quick disappearing act when being incorporated or in custards that rely on its highly available gluten. Manufacturers differ in the wording on the label.

If you have a choice, buy a good quality vanilla . It is used here as a basic tool in granting complexity to the flavour of sugar, and I use a lot of it. If all you can get is a common supermarket brand, transfer it to a larger bottle and add a small amount of fine Cognac and a vanilla bean to improve the flavour.

Finally, a word about the food colouring, used here in chocolate decorations and tiles. Since even a few drops of water can cause chocolate to seize up and become grainy, the highly concentrated commercial paste or powder dyes are essential to creating deep, rich hues. (Paste colours added in large amounts will also cause chocolate to seize, and this can be remedied up to a point by whisking in a small amount of oil – not butter, which contains its own moisture.) Commercial colouring products are available in cake decorating supply shops. If you are restricted to liquid food colouring you will be limited to a pastel palette.

TECHNIQUE NOTES
To break chocolate, use a heavy, blunt, thick-bladed chef's knife: press the tip straight down into the block, then slowly bring the handle down so the blade acts as a wedge and the chocolate breaks.

To melt chocolate, which scorches easily, use the lowest temperature possible. If you inadvertently scorch the chocolate you can still save the good part by shaking it undisturbed through a strainer while still warm. Since the bowl used to melt chocolate is usually used again in the next step, these recipes employ a simple set-up of 'bowl over saucepan a quarter full of simmering water' instead of a double boiler for melting, (see Equipment Notes.) Be sure they fit together well to prevent steam from contaminating the chocolate – water is as great a hazard as high heat.

For dipping remember you must always melt more chocolate than you will use so you will have enough to immerse each object. Just cool and store any leftovers.

This brings us to the tempering controversy. The rather alarming whitish surface you sometimes find on chocolate is not from moisture or even old age - it results when the wrong one of two possible configurations of fat crystals forms, usually encouraged by starting at too high a heat and cooling too rapidly. Since it requires the psychic powers of an experienced chocolatier to avoid completely, and is of concern here only in the area of dipped sweets when they are to be kept for a long time, I will not attempt to explore its subtleties. Rest assured that the crystals do not affect flavour or quality, and chocolate so afflicted can be re-melted and used again with confidence.

Prepare nuts according to their type. Pecans and walnuts can be used as they are, but hazelnuts and almonds need to have their skins removed. In the case of hazelnuts this is done by toasting them on a baking sheet in a 180°C/350°F/Gas 4 oven for about 10 minutes until they are golden and the skins are loose. Cool them, then rub a few at a time between your palms, holding your hands apart at the bottom so the skins drop out.

Almonds have to be blanched. It is easier to buy them blanched than to do it yourself, but if you wish to, pour boiling water over them and soak until cool, then squeeze each nut to slip from its skin. Almonds should then also be toasted before use, again, on a baking sheet in a 180°C/350°F/Gas 4 oven for 10 minutes (longer if you have just soaked the nuts). I also toast pistachios to crisp them: this is to no avail unless you then rub them in a tea towel to remove the excess oil.

Three other basic techniques must be correct to ensure success with these recipes: creaming butter and sugar, whisking egg whites and folding. If you are creaming butter and sugar by hand, the butter you start with must be soft enough not to leave lumps but firm enough to avoid melting. The food processor used in recipes here is far more forgiving of cold butter, but one can still risk melting by overprocessing, since friction produced by the blade generates its own heat.

Whisking egg whites is one of the trickiest and most important proceedures. The greatest danger lies in over-beating, causing a dry, crumbling texture that is difficult to fold smoothly. The more sugar used in the given recipe, the longer this stage is forestalled – but one must learn visually when to stop whisking in a range of instances.

Folding is a technique uniquely important in dessert work, yet often the downfall of even many would-be professionals. The process is usually one of combining powdered, ground or liquid ingredients with a mixture into which a great deal of air has been whisked. Since this mixture is likely to be losing its volume anyway from the moment you've stopped whisking it, you want to disturb it only as much as is necessary to combine the elements. What you are doing, then, as opposed to stirring, is dragging ingredients through sticky bubbles to cling evenly to them in the wake of your rubber spatula. Plunge the spatula in at a 45° angle just right of centre in your bowl, proceed downwards to the left at that angle, then follow the contour of the bowl up again at the opposite side of the bowl, flipping the mixture you bring up with you over the top. Repeat as you rotate the bowl by quarter turns.

As a last word of warning from the voice of experience – always set a timer for everything you put in an oven or leave on a hob.

The Desserts

Chevron Strawberries

Stemmed strawberries dipped in white and dark chocolate.

EQUIPMENT
Kitchen scales
Kitchen towels
2 small bowls
Small saucepan
Whisk
Brush for cleaning berries
Baking parchment lined baking sheet
Small strong freezer bag
Rubber spatula

This striking presentation came about as I tried to dress up huge succulent stemmed strawberries. I combined the two types of coating since they're both so good with the berries, and also both so good with each other. Served from a buffet or several on a plate as dessert, these strawberries are as well received in corporate boardrooms as they were at my family reunion barbecue. The simple contrasting squiggle makes a strong graphic statement well worth that final step.

Try to dip these within a few hours of serving. They should be kept in a cool place but preferably not refrigerated, since they tend to sweat when restored to room temperature. The moisture marks the chocolate and loosens the berry, in which case the chocolate stays behind when the fruit is picked up.

The stems make convenient handles, but if only normal clipped-stem berries are available, it has been my experience that people will find a way to convey them to their mouths.

Serves: 20 dipped strawberries, if good sized and served on plates, serves perhaps 6; more as part of a buffet.

INGREDIENTS:

250 g/8 oz white chocolate (more, if dipping bowl is shallow)
250 g/8 oz dark chocolate (more, if dipping bowl is shallow)
20 large strawberries with leaves and stems

INSTRUCTIONS:

Melt the white chocolate in a small bowl over saucepan a quarter full of simmering water. Whisk until smooth. While the chocolate is melting brush the berries clean, if necessary. If you have to rinse them, lay them on kitchen towels and make sure they are absolutely dry before you continue.

Hold a strawberry by its stem and dip into the white chocolate at a 45° angle with the most attractive side of the berry towards you. Watch the progress of the edge of chocolate across the side of the berry until it is halfway up on a diagonal. Lift out of the chocolate, shake slightly to remove the excess and turn it so the good side points up, then scrape the underside across the edge of the bowl. Transfer to a baking parchment covered baking sheet. If too much chocolate pools round the base of the berry, you may need to add a few drops of vegetable oil to the chocolate to thin it. Repeat with the remaining berries.

When all the berries have been dipped put them in a cool place for a few minutes to set the chocolate. In another small bowl melt the dark chocolate over simmering water. Whisk until smooth.

Hold the berry with the side towards you but at opposite angle from that used the first time. Dip quickly into the dark chocolate and shake lightly but do not scrape before setting back on the baking sheet. When all are done return the berries to the cool place to set the chocolate.

Re-melt the remaining white chocolate in a bowl over the pan. Scrape the white chocolate into a strong freezer bag, cut small hole at the corner and pipe a line across the face of each berry.

About keeping: Will keep in a cool place for a few hours.

Mexican Chocolate Custard Cake

A dessert halfway between a cake and a custard, served with exotic and other fresh fruit; accompanied with whipped cream or *crème fraîche* and a dash of cinnamon.

EQUIPMENT:
Thin bladed knife

One of the great disappointments of my earliest travels was the pastry of Spain. Perhaps the result of 700 years of Moorish occupation or, more likely, the lack of dairy farming in this arid land, the offerings were typically huge, greasy, dry and tasteless. Mexico has largely inherited the same lacklustre repertoire, except for this inspired creation. It is a contribution to the joys of chocolate that may well cancel all the sins of other Mexican pastries and those of the mother country, too. Halfway between a cake and a pudding, this suspended mass of moist dark chocolate and nuts is also halfway to heaven. A simple slice of this cake is the ideal focus of a composed plate, served with a selection of exotic and other fresh fruit and a dollop of whipped cream or *crème fraîche*, or set among alternative accompaniments as listed at right.

Serves: 10

INGREDIENTS:

1 recipe Chocolate Custard Cake (4)
1 recipe Whipped Cream (25) or
*   Whipped Crème Fraîche (26)*
Dash of ground cinnamon
2-3 papayas, skinned and sliced
1 kg/2 lb strawberries, brushed or
*   washed and dried*
1 large cantaloupe or honeydew
*   melon, sliced and skin removed*

INSTRUCTIONS:

Cut the cake in 2-2.5 cm/¼-1 in slices and lay on a plate. Dollop with whipped cream or *crème fraîche*, dust with cinnamon and surround with prepared fruit.

About keeping: Once composed, serve immediately.

Also try: Serve with a dollop of Tangerine Curd (22) folded with 250 ml/8 fl oz of whipped cream. The cake could also become the centre of a formal plate, set in a pool of Vanilla Custard (31) and piped with a zigzag of Bitter Orange Sauce (28), Raspberry Sauce (29) or Apricot Sauce (30). Add a scattering of fresh berries.

Lightning Bolt Dacquoise

Hazelnut meringue layered with coffee buttercream, covered with dark chocolate ganache and tinted, drawn and gilded white chocolate tiles.

EQUIPMENT:
Ruler
Serrated knife
Baking parchment
Piping bag with
  5 cm/2 in wide
  flat pastry filling
  nozzle
Thick paper for
  templates
Scalpel

This no-holds-barred showstopper may be too abstract for some – that is, until they taste it. This dacquoise gained its snazzy skin when I realized that the smooth seams chocolate tiles would provide on a cake could make the edge piping I hate unnecessary. The designer in me stirred – a chance to ignore entirely the fact that it's a cake!

The first incarnation of this torte was as a Christmas gift box with edible ribbons made as a favour to an old client. Another time it became a set of 15 cakes in smeared pastels and musical notes atop a chocolate grand piano, reached through a forest of suspended star cookies and chocolate sheet music on stands. More recently, I've done a Valentine box with hot-pink hearts all over it.

I must admit the design here is not for the beginner, but it showcases what beautiful and unique effects can be had with as little as one sheet of chocolate and a little imagination. In any case, it's easier than it looks, and the amazed reactions of guests are a lot of fun.

Serves: 20

NOTES:

Although the whole is complex the four parts are relatively easy to make days ahead. The yield is large – you may want to freeze part of the meringue-and-buttercream cake to cover differently another time.

INGREDIENTS:

1 recipe Almond-Hazelnut
  Meringue (5)
1 recipe Coffee Buttercream (16)
1 recipe Dark Chocolate Ganache
  (24)
1 recipe marbled white Chocolate
  Tiles (40B)
1 recipe tinted Chocolate Tiles
  (40), one end gilded

INSTRUCTIONS:

Trim the edges of the meringue layer to a 40 x 28 cm/16 x 11 in rectangle with a serrated knife. Cut again to make four strips 10 x 28 cm/4 x 11 in. Lay the strips on baking parchment on the back of a baking sheet and dry them in a 180°C/350°F/Gas 4 oven for 10–15 minutes until they are crisp but not darkened. Cool completely.

Place one strip face down in front of you and pipe on a layer of coffee buttercream. Lay another strip on top, and repeat the sequence until all four strips are filled and stacked. You can wrap and refrigerate the dacquoise at this point and prepare your tiles and ganache – or even freeze it for later completion.

Make a full-scale drawing on thick paper of your design for the three sides of the cake you need to cover, allowing an extra 5 mm/¼ in at the seams for the thickness of the ganache. With a scalpel cut the paper along the lines of your drawing to form patterns for each piece you will need, then cut them out of the appropriate chocolate sheet.

Lay the torte on its side in front of you and pipe on a layer of chocolate ganache, making sure it is cool enough not to run. Put on the tiles. Turn it over and cover the other side of the ganache and tiles. Finally set it upright and pipe the top with ganache, fitting the top tile pieces to form a flush edge with the sides, and press into place.

About keeping: If wrapped tightly in cling film this torte can be refrigerated, but return it to room temperature before unwrapping or the moisture condensation may cause the colours to run. Room temperature is also the ideal temperature for serving since the torte will be easier to cut (use a thin-bladed knife and simply push through) and the flavours will be better. It will keep in the refrigerator for several days.

Also try: Cover with White Chocolate Ganache (23); or use either the White or Dark Chocolate Ganache (24) with appliques of Chocolate Decorations (43) instead of Chocolate Tiles.

Chocolate Tortellini in Pear Syrup

Fanned poached pear half with ricotta and chestnut filled chocolate tortellini in reduced Chardonnay and Armagnac pear syrup. Chocolate-dipped anisette biscuits on the side.

EQUIPMENT:
Kitchen scales
Small bowl over
 small saucepan
Whisk
Baking parchment
 lined baking sheet
Large saucepan
Pasta pot

I had long despaired the wasting of gallons of delicious but useless wine based liquid in which I've poached pears, and sought a way to salvage it. I had also long considered dessert pasta to be where *nouvelle cuisine* scrapes the bottom of the barrel – but when it met my poaching liquid, something happened. The bitter chocolate dough with the nutty cheese filling, the hot aromatic pear poaching liquid, fruit and crispy biscuit together become a dessert far more wonderful than the mere sum of its parts – and a drop-dead visual treat as well.

Serves: 6

NOTES:

Poached pears should be made a day or more ahead to allow the flavour of the liquid to develop.

INGREDIENTS:

125 g/4 oz dark chocolate
12 Italian anisette biscuits
Liquid broth and 6 pear halves
 from 2 recipes Poached Pears
 (34), see Notes at left
1 recipe Chocolate Tortellini (10)
2 tablespoons Armagnac or other
 fine Cognac

INSTRUCTIONS:

Melt the chocolate in a small bowl over a saucepan a quarter full of simmering water. Whisk until smooth. Dip one end of each of the biscuits in the chocolate. Lay the biscuits on a parchment-covered baking sheet and put in a cool place to set.

Drain the poaching liquid from pears into a large saucepan. You will be starting with about 2 litres/ 3¼ pints; reduce this to 1.5 litres/ 2½ pints. At a full boil this takes 10-15 minutes.

Cook the Chocolate Tortellini in a large pasta pot half full of boiling water until they are *al dente*. Drain them, then add to reduced pear syrup along with the Armagnac.

Heat soup bowls. Fan-cut six pears and lay a pear half at the side of each bowl. Ladle in the syrup and tortellini. Serve with the biscuits on the side.

About keeping: Pasta must be cooked close to serving time; the dough will lose its texture if it remains in the syrup for long, especially if kept warm.

Also try: Sprinkle with a dusting of Spiced Ground Orange Peel (41).

Chocolate Pastry Latticed Apricot Tart

Apricot, almond and brandy filling in a chocolate pastry crust.

EQUIPMENT:
Pastry board
Rolling pin
23 cm/9 in flan tin
Pastry wheel
Paring knife

This attractive presentation turns the humble standby tart into a fitting dessert for a simple meal or a formal one. The chocolate pastry is flexible enough to allow the dense weaving of pastry strips that defines a true lattice-topped tart. Besides their rich colour and concentrated flavour, the apricots' texture and density provide a firm base that supports the lattice and allows the tart to hold its shape well when cut. Since apricots' bulk and flavour survive processing they are the only fruit I still buy in cans, one to be enjoyed in winter when fresh choices are limited.

Serves: 8

INGREDIENTS:

1 recipe Chocolate Pastry (6)
1 recipe Apricot Pie Filling (17)
½ recipe Whipped Cream (25)

INSTRUCTIONS:

Lightly dust a pastry board or work surface and the first piece of dough with flour, then roll out into a circle. Fold the dough into quarters, place in the flan tin and unfold. Add the filling. Roll out the second piece of dough and cut into 2.5 cm/1 in strips with a pastry wheel.

Lay parallel strips 2.5 cm/1 in apart across the top of the tart; trim the ends. Fold alternating strips more than halfway back on themselves, then lay a strip across the centre perpendicular to the first set of strips. Flip the folded strips back across the tart, then fold back the alternate strips: lay in each additional strip to the edge of the tart, then from the centre to the opposite edge of the tart. Trim the end of all the strips, and fold the overhang of the bottom crust up over them.

Bake at 180°C/350°F/Gas 4 for 50 minutes or until the filling begins to bubble up round the edges. Cool completely before serving. Serve with a dollop of whipped cream.

About keeping: Can be frozen before being baked. You may keep for up to one day after baking before serving.

Mango and Chocolate Sorbets

Creamy sorbets of mango and chocolate, served with a chocolate-covered spoon; decorated with a dark chocolate ribbon.

EQUIPMENT:
Kitchen scales
Small bowl over
 small saucepan
6 dessertspoons
Baking parchment
 lined baking sheet
Ice cream scoop
6 stemmed glasses
 or bowls

A colleague and friend once said 'the raspberry may be the queen of fruit, but mango is the king'. In any case both fruits find their match in chocolate. Here the lush tropical intensity of the mango is complemented by the cool, slightly bitter iciness of chocolate in sorbet form, so unlike chocolate ice cream – it reminds me more of iced Thai coffee. The chocolate-dipped spoon is an accent bound to be remembered.

Serves: 6

INGREDIENTS:

*125 g/4 oz dark chocolate for
  spoons
1 recipe Chocolate Sorbet (38)
1 recipe Mango Sorbet (39)
½ recipe Chocolate Decorations
  (43) in dark chocolate*

INSTRUCTIONS:

Melt the chocolate in a small bowl over a saucepan a quarter full of simmering water. Whisk until smooth. Dip the spoons in the chocolate: to get the drip effect, turn the spoon upright in mid drip. Set on a baking parchment lined baking sheet and put in cool place to set. Refrigerate them briefly, if you will be using them soon.

Scoop the sorbets into stemmed glasses or bowls, then twist a length of dark chocolate ribbon over the top and serve with the chocolate covered spoon.

About keeping: Will keep, frozen, for up to 3 months.

Also try: Both sorbets are also good with Raspberry Sauce (29).

Custard-filled Chocolate Chip Eclairs

Spiral-piped eclairs flecked with chocolate bits, filled with chocolate custard and topped with chocolate-Cognac sauce and crystallized violets.

EQUIPMENT
1 large piping bag
  with no nozzle

The French have long recognized the natural affinity of chocolate and pastry, from chocolate croissants to the simple treat of *pain au chocolat*. This pairing of crisp, rich, eggy choux pastry with flecks of chocolate brings that happy marriage to the realm of the eclair.

Serves: 6

INGREDIENTS:

*1 recipe Chocolate Chip Eclairs
  (11)
1 recipe Chocolate Custard Filling
  (20)
½ recipe Chocolate-Cognac
  Sauce (27)
Crystallized violets*

INSTRUCTIONS:

Slit the eclairs lengthways from the cut edge and remove any soft dough that remains inside. Fill the piping bag with the custard, then fill each eclair. Place an eclair on each plate. Pour a stream of chocolate sauce in a zigzag pattern across each eclair and out to the edge of the centre of the plate. Decorate with crystallized violets.

This sauce is liquid at slightly warmer than room temperature; if it is the proper consistency it will pour beautifully, yet set slightly on the plate and not spread.

About keeping: Serve immediately once the dessert is assembled.

Also try: This dessert invites many variations. Substitute Vanilla Custard Filling (19), Whipped Cream (25) or Tangerine Curd (22) folded with 250 ml/8 fl oz plain whipped cream. Or use either of the custard fillings lightened as for Layered Custard Cream Parfaits (52) half the recipe of the custard folded with three quarters of the recipe for Whipped Cream (25), which uses 180 ml/6 fl oz cream, before whipping, plus the vanilla and cream that suit the custards. Could also be drizzled with Raspberry Sauce (29) rather than Chocolate-Cognac Sauce (27).

Chocolate Chip-Mint Ice Cream Sandwiches

Cakey chocolate biscuits filled with home-made chocolate chip-mint ice cream, decorated with fresh mint and served in a sandwich bag.

EQUIPMENT:
Warm serrated
 knife
10 cm/4 in
 sandwich bags
 and seals

A *trompe l'oeil* sandwich of ice cream and biscuits served in a sandwich bag may at first appear destined for a school lunch box, then, on second glance, more appropriate to being packed in ice on its way to a family picnic. But the cakey home-made biscuits and exquisite home-made chocolate chip-mint ice cream wouldn't be unwelcome on even the most formal plate. In fact, there in particular it might be quite fun. The ice cream recipe is based on one we made at my grandparents' farm in northern Wisconsin on hot August afternoons. Even with 12 cousins to take turns on the handle it seemed to take forever to make. With the modern freezer compartment ice cream makers, you don't even have to sweat and it tastes almost as good.

Serves: 8

NOTES:

For this formal presentation I have improved the appearance of a sandwich bag by fastening it with a gold adhesive seal. The stickers avidly collected by children could provide a host of other decorative possibilities.

INGREDIENTS:

1 recipe Chocolate Chip-Mint Ice
 Cream (37)
1 recipe Chocolate Sandwich
 Biscuits (7)
Fresh mint sprigs

INSTRUCTIONS:

Although home-made ice creams are very dense and usually become much firmer than commercial brands when stored in the freezer, you will still have to work quickly. Loosen the ice cream from the square plastic containers and cut into eight 1-2 cm/$\frac{1}{2}$-$\frac{3}{4}$ in slices. As you layer each slice between two biscuits, cut the completed sandwich in half diagonally with serrated knife, then wrap and store in the freezer. These can be served any time after they have become firm. Decorate each with a fresh mint sprig.

About keeping: The biscuits can be made several days before assembly; the ice cream should be made at least a day ahead to allow it to freeze solidly before slicing. If the sandwiches are to be kept for some time after assembly, tuck each inside an extra, freezerproof sandwich bag.

Also try: Layer the biscuits with Mango Sorbet (39), or if you prefer quarter them and serve at room temperature as a sandwich biscuit filled with Coffee Buttercream (16) or Whiskey-Apricot Filling (15).

Whiskey-Apricot Chocolate Torte

Chocolate torte
with whiskey-
apricot filling,
glazed with
chocolate ganache
and decorated with
a moulded column

EQUIPMENT:
Long thin bladed
 serrated knife
Metal flan or cake
 tin base or cardboard
Piping bag fitted
 with 5 cm/2 in
 wide filling nozzle
Palette knife

This incarnation of the classic 'flourless' dark chocolate torte, the same component as used in the Chocolate-Chocolate Mousse Torte, is close in spirit to the original Viennese Sachertorte. However, replacing the sticky sweet jam or preserve filling with this chunky, sharp apricot filling achieves a deeply satisfying balance between fruit and chocolate, and one that is accessible all year long. It is simple, yet rich and elegant.

Serves: 16

NOTES:

A traditional decoration might be a single swirl of icing, a monogram or a fan of chocolate filigree. Here an unusual custom-made mould filled with tinted white chocolate becomes the accent that steals the show, but such an accent could be anything on this sumptuous stage – an off-centre row of moulded apricot roses or any decoration you choose. To use a chocolate mould, melt tinted or plain chocolate (see Ingredients Notes) in a bowl over simmering water; fill the mould, then allow it to cool and pop out the chocolate.

INGREDIENTS:

1 recipe Dark Chocolate Torte (l)
1 recipe Whiskey-Apricot Filling (15)
1 recipe Dark Chocolate Ganache (24)
Any moulded white chocolate decoration (or decoration of your choice from the Accents and Decorations section)

INSTRUCTIONS:

This cake both rises and falls to alarming levels. You did nothing wrong, but you will have to trim the hour-glass shaped overhang to a smooth edge. Don't waste those tasty scraps! With a long serrated knife carefully slice the cake horizontally into two equal layers. Slide a flan or cake tin base or cardboard into the cut, and remove the top layer.

Fill a piping bag with the apricot filling and pipe evenly on to the first layer of cake. You may have to pry the icing nozzle open a bit to accommodate the chunks of fruit. Slide the top layer off its tray on to the filling. When the ganache is cool enough not to run, ice the sides first. Then, using a palette knife, scrape the remaining ganache on top, smooth to cover and make a final swirl in a fan pattern. If using a moulded decoration like the one pictured, be sure to put it in place before the ganache sets.

About keeping: This torte will keep for up to a week, iced and refrigerated, though the ganache will lose its lustre under refrigeration. Return to room temperature before serving.

For eight or fewer guests cut the un-iced torte in half; freeze the other half to ice another time, it can be frozen for several months.

Also try: This could also be covered with white Chocolate Tiles (40), much like the Lightning Bolt Dacquoise, or with White Chocolate Ganache (23).

Raspberries with Custard and Fruit Sauce

A scattering of red and golden raspberries in a pool of custard that's piped with red raspberry and apricot sauce squiggles; accented with tinted, striped and zigzagged white chocolate tiles.

EQUIPMENT:
Measuring jug or 60 ml/2 fl oz ladle
2 small, strong freezer bags

The presentation here may be one of the most fantastic in the book, but it is also one of the simplest: fruit with fruit sauce, custard and chocolate. Rarity is provided by the golden raspberries. If you have never tasted them and have the opportunity, don't miss it. The experience is of raspberryness magnified – at once sweeter and more piquant. Fragile by nature, these berries rarely make it to the shops. When they do, the event is worth celebrating. They are grown in Scotland, but are usually only available at specialist greengrocers.

Serves: 8

NOTES:

For those intimidated by the precision cut of chocolate tiles elsewhere in this book, here's a treatment that can't go wrong.

INGREDIENTS:

1 recipe Vanilla Custard (31)
½ recipe Raspberry Sauce (29)
½ recipe Apricot Sauce (30)
500 g/1 lb fresh red raspberries
500 g/1 lb fresh golden raspberries, strawberries or blueberries
1 recipe tinted white, striped and zigzagged Chocolate Tiles (40C)

INSTRUCTIONS:

Pour about 60 ml/2 fl oz custard sauce on each plate, tilting to cover. This will usually be enough to coat the centre of a standard 25 cm/10 in dinner plate. Test it. If the custard is too deep, the piped sauce will sink and slip from view.

Put each fruit sauce in its own freezer bag and cut a small hole in one corner. Squirt a squiggle of each sauce across the custard. Scatter liberally with berries and decorate with broken pieces of striped and drawn white chocolate tile.

About keeping: Serve immediately after assembling.

Also try: Use strawberries and blueberries with Bitter Orange Sauce (28) instead of the apricot sauce. Try other seasonal combinations.

Meringue and Chocolate Chequerboard

Squares of hazelnut meringue covered with dark chocolate ganache and tinted white chocolate tiles in alternating colours; topped with chocolate mousse and tangerine curd, berries and edible blossoms.

EQUIPMENT:
Kitchen scales
Ruler
Serrated knife
Palette knife
30 x 42.5 x 2.5cm/
  12 x 17 x 2 in Swiss
  roll tin
Scalpel
2 piping bags with
  5 cm/2 in wide,
  flat filling nozzles,
  1 with star nozzle
  for optional garnishes

A dessert buffet can be a sound logistical solution, presented on its own with coffee in a new location, to offer a sweet late in a cocktail hors d'oeuvre party, at a buffet supper or even after a sit-down dinner, when clearing the debris away to serve dessert can be daunting. It is also a way of achieving an elaborate display without taking the last-minute time to compose individual plates, and there are many ways to customize it for different effects. Once I even piped these squares with chocolate ganache alphabet letters, rather than this florid display.

Serves: 20 people, two squares apiece

INGREDIENTS:

1 recipe Almond-Hazelnut
  Meringue (5)
½ recipe tinted white Chocolate
  Tiles (40)
½ recipe tinted white Chocolate
  Tiles (40) in contrasting colour
1½ recipes Dark Chocolate
  Ganache (24)
½ recipe (125 g/4 oz) Dark
  Chocolate Mousse (13)
¼ recipe (125 g/4 oz)
  Tangerine Curd (22)
Other garnishes, including edible
  blossoms, berries and silver ball
  decorations

INSTRUCTIONS:

Trim the edges of the meringue layer to a 40 x 25 cm/16 x 10 in rectangle using a ruler and a serrated knife. Score and slice the rectangle into 5 cm/2 in squares. Place on the back of a baking sheet and dry in a 180°C/ 350°F/ Gas 4 oven for 10 minutes, until the meringue is crisp but not darkened. Cool.

Meanwhile, using a ruler and scalpel cut the two colours of chocolate tiles into 5 cm/2 in squares. Put the chocolate ganache in a piping bag fitted with filling nozzle, and cover several meringue squares at a time with the ganache. Use a palette knife to separate the chocolate tile squares from the baking parchment and place them on the ganache – press lightly to secure. Cover half the total number of squares with each colour and arrange in a chequerboard design for serving. Pipe with rosettes of mousse and curd, and top with a random selection of decorations.

About keeping: These squares can be wrapped and stored for a few days but are best enjoyed soon after completion.

Also try: Vary the combinations of tinted tiles. Pipe with Chocolate Custard Filling (20) or Vanilla Custard Filling (19), or add small scoops of Spiced Mascarpone (14).

Chocolate-Chocolate Mousse Torte

Chocolate torte layered with chocolate mousse and fresh raspberries, topped with whipped cream; served with raspberry sauce.

EQUIPMENT:
Long, thin bladed
 serrated knife
Flan or cake tin
 base or cardboard
 cake round
Cake plate with
 25 cm/10 in flat
 base
Rubber spatula
Palette knife
Cling film
Piping bag with
 large star nozzle

This title is more descriptive than redundant - a double dose of dense, moist chocolate torte filled and topped with a slightly creamy yet airy and dry-textured chocolate mousse. The filling layer is studded with raspberries, whose sharp flavour balances well with the richness of cake and mousse; the whipped cream round the sides provides the cake with a self-contained decoration that lightens the overall effect. In my restaurant experience this torte was the mainstay of my repertoire. It has even been the choice of a pair of engaged chocaholics for their wedding cake!

Serves: 12

INGREDIENTS:

1 recipe Dark Chocolate Torte (1)
1 recipe Dark Chocolate Mousse
 (13)
500 g/1 lb fresh raspberries
1 recipe Whipped Cream (25)
1 recipe Raspberry Sauce (29),
 optional

INSTRUCTIONS:

Trim the overhanging torte edges and treat yourself to the scraps. Carefully slice the cake horizontally into two equal layers with a long serrated knife. Because this is essentially a flourless cake there is little gluten to bind it, and it will be crumbly and very delicate. Slide a flan or cake tin base or cardboard into the bottom, and lift off the top layer. Slide the bottom layer onto the cake plate. Any breaks will eventually be cemented by the mousse when it sets.

Before assembly the mousse should be chilled for about 2 hours from the time it was made, or until not yet set but no longer runny. Lift half of the mousse on to the first cake layer using a rubber spatula. Smooth with a palette knife, taking care to disturb the texture of the mousse as little as possible. Scatter the raspberries over the surface, and press them in lightly. Invert the top cake layer and spread with a small amount of the remaining mousse, flip it over on to the raspberries and smooth the sides with a palette knife. Spread the remaining mousse on top and

smooth with the palette knife after running it under hot water. Wrap the sides in cling film to retain the torte's shape and refrigerate until firm.

Once firm, the torte can be wrapped and frozen for several weeks.

Pipe strips of whipped cream from the base to top all the way round the chilled cake, topping with a row of rosettes round the top edge. Top the cake with remaining berries or reserve them for a plate decoration. Serve with raspberry sauce if you like.

About keeping: Refrigerate. Serve within 8 hours once whipped cream is piped.

Also try: This torte will stand on its own merits without raspberries. Try spreading the first layer with Whiskey-Apricot Filling (15) before adding the first layer of mousse, or just use the mousse alone.

Chocolate Pancakes with Flambéed Oranges

Chocolate pancakes filled with fresh orange chunks flambéed in Grand Marnier, topped with whipped cream and spiced ground orange peel.

EQUIPMENT:
Piping bag with 5 cm/2 in wide, flat filling nozzle

The idea developed here surfaced in the search for a succulent, fruity winter dessert. Oranges, unfortunately are rarely used in desserts as themselves. Cut as they are in this dish to minimise tough pulp, and flambéed in liqueur to intensify their flavour, they are quite transformed. When this dish was served to 150 people at a formal dinner, every plate returned from the dining room scraped clean.

Serves: 6

INGREDIENTS:

1 recipe Flambéed Oranges (18)
1 recipe Chocolate Pancakes (12)
1 recipe Whipped Cream (25)
1 recipe Spiced Ground Orange Peel (41)

INSTRUCTIONS:

Place approximately 45 g/1½ oz flambéed oranges in the centre of the longer two thirds of a pancake. Fold the upper edge one third down over the oranges, then fold in each side so it becomes an envelope with the open flap towards you, spilling out oranges.

Place two composed pancakes on each plate. Decorate with three folds of whipped cream piped with the wide, flat filling nozzle and a sprinkling of ground orange peel.

About keeping: Serve immediately.

Also try: Spread a tablespoon or two of Spiced Mascarpone (14) on to the pancakes under the oranges before you fill them. You can also replace the whipped cream with Whipped *Crème Fraîche* (26).

Chocolate Ribbon Cake

Chocolate génoise layered with chocolate custard and nectarines, iced with white chocolate ganache and pastel chocolate decorations.

EQUIPMENT:
Baking parchment
Ruler
Serrated knife
Cling film
Piping bag with
 5 cm/2 in wide,
 flat filling nozzle
Palette knife

This outrageous presentation – a showcase for the potential of chocolate decorations – cloaks my most basic cake, which is just as good, believe it or not, without its finery. A simple chocolate sponge cake and chocolate custard filling can be paired with a full cavalcade of peak-season fruit all summer long; in this case, nectarines. The chocolate decorations are a flexible medium that opens a realm of possibilities completely different from that of the chocolate tiles and can have enormous impact.

Serves: 14

NOTES:

The three mixtures used here may take time, but they last for months in the refrigerator. And making the cut-outs, once you get to it, is more purely child's play than any other form of expression in the discipline.

In this assembly one of the four strips of *génoise* will be left over. Actually I've found that a bit extra of something is extremely useful in the making of single whole desserts like this, which offer absolutely no way to snitch a bit before serving; the excess will help keep impatient hands from the masterpiece until the guests are served.

Your use of decorations may make the cake difficult to cut; in this case, remove sections of the design to decorate the plates as you serve.

INGREDIENTS:

1 recipe Chocolate Génoise (3)
1 recipe Chocolate Custard Filling (20)
3-4 nectarines, peeled and sliced
1 recipe White Chocolate Ganache (23)
3 recipes Chocolate Decorations (43)

INSTRUCTIONS:

Flip the génoise on to baking parchment on a work surface. Trim the edges to form a 40 x 28 cm/16 x 11 in rectangle using a ruler and serrated knife.

Lay one strip on a serving tray. If you want to avoid cleaning areas round the cake later, cover them with cling film. Fill a piping bag fitted with a 5 cm/2 in wide filling nozzle with chocolate custard, and pipe a layer on to the cake. Add the nectarine slices end to end lengthwise, so you will cut across them when slicing. Pipe a thin layer of custard on the next cake strip and flip it over on top of the nectarines. Repeat. Wrap the cake tightly with cling film and refrigerate for a few hours or up to one day before continuing. During this time, prepare the chocolate decorations, one batch in each of the colours, and the white chocolate ganache.

If the ganache has been made in advance and re-melted, it may need to be refrigerated again to reach the proper piping texture. When it is ready, fill a piping bag, again fitted with a 5 cm/2 in wide filling nozzle, and cover the cake on the sides and top; smooth with a palette knife that has been warmed under hot water.

Work, roll and cut the chocolate decorations as explained in the component recipe (page 105). Press the decorations into place. To simplify slicing, remove sections of ribbon as you cut and add to the plates as the cake is served.

About keeping: Keep the cake in a cool place until serving. Although many of the elements are forgiving while unassembled, the finished cake should be eaten within a few hours of completion.

Also try: Fill with Vanilla Custard Filling (19) and other fruit or even with Spiced Mascarpone (14). Ice by piping with Whipped Cream (25) or Whipped *Crème Fraîche* (26).

Mocha Mousse with Bitter Orange Sauce

Mocha and vanilla custard cream mousses layered in a mould; served with bitter orange sauce.

EQUIPMENT:
Bowl of hot water for loosening mousse from mould

This was a case where the mould came first, then the moulded. Photographer Patricia Brabant found this particularly fine and unusual antique crockery mould, which led me to find a use for it. I was already well out of my jelly phase but have always loved the drama of a moulded dessert. The separation of leaf and flower inspired this two-toned beauty, a dense Bavarian-style jellied mocha mousse and matching layer of vanilla cream meant to melt in the mouth while the essences of coffee, chocolate, cream and orange mingle together.

Serves: 6

N O T E S :

Never having used a crockery mould before, I was surprised to find I prefer it to metal. Since its absorption of heat is more subtle, or perhaps because of a slicker surface, it releases the filling more easily with detail intact and a minimum of hot-water dunking.

I N G R E D I E N T S :

1 recipe Moulded Mocha and Cream Mousse (35)
1 recipe Bitter Orange Sauce (28)

I N S T R U C T I O N S :

Quickly dip the base of the mould in hot water to loosen the contents. Invert on to a serving plate and unmould; you may have to pull at the edge to free the mousse from the vacuum. Surround with bitter orange sauce.

About keeping: Will keep, refrigerated, for several days before unmoulding.

Also try: Use individual moulds or ramekins. It is also excellent served with Raspberry Sauce (29).

Fruit and Cream with Chocolate Triangles

Tinted, dark-spattered white chocolate triangles and whipped *crème fraîche*; with strawberries, kiwi fruit and cantaloupe cubes in melon liqueur, decorated with fresh mint.

EQUIPMENT:
Ruler
Scalpel
Paring knife

When I first began experimenting with white chocolate sheets I was intrigued by the idea of using them to create a three dimensional effect by standing them up. Then a caterer friend delivered the challenge of creating a dessert for his first major sit-down dinner – a light spring meal for 70 people. This was the result – a simple plate of fruit and cream updated. The sweet white chocolate is countered by the sour whipped *crème fraîche*. Only the melon is treated, here – cut in cubes (so they wouldn't roll around on the plate!), soaked in melon liqueur and decorated with finely sliced fresh mint leaves.

Serves: 6

INGREDIENTS:

1 recipe tinted white Chocolate Tiles with dark chocolate drizzle (40A)
1 recipe Whipped Crème Fraîche *(26)*
500 g/1 lb strawberries, brushed or, if necessary, rinsed and thoroughly dried
3 kiwi fruit, skinned and sliced
Cubes of cantaloupe, doused with melon liqueur
Mint leaves cut in very thin strips

INSTRUCTIONS:

Cut the chocolate tile sheet into triangles measured to fit your plates, using a ruler and scalpel.

Spoon a dollop of whipped *crème fraîche* in the centre of each plate and push three chocolate triangles into each from the side, so they stand upright. Scatter the fruit between the chocolate triangles and decorate the melon cubes with the mint.

About keeping: Serve immediately after assembling.

Also try: Any complementary combination of fresh seasonal fruit.

The Tomlin Tart

Individual chocolate pastry cases filled with vanilla custard, topped with fresh figs, kiwi fruit and papaya and glazed with apple jelly.

EQUIPMENT:
Kitchen scales
Fork
Paring knife
Small melon baller
Small saucepan
Small pastry brush

While visiting friends once in Los Angeles I found out that Lily Tomlin needed a chef to cook for the writers and household during the production of her next TV special. It was decided that I would 'audition' by preparing some special dish – but what? Since I was leaving the next day and had to deliver my dish before Lily went out that evening, I had one afternoon. Desserts were already my forte then, but the place I was staying was ill-equipped to produce what I was used to. There was, however, a garden fig tree heavily laden with perfect, ripe fruit. These fresh fruit tarts were the result. Despite great difficulty finding the house, including a brief altercation with LA police, I arrived in time for introductions but not for tasting. On return to San Francisco the next evening I got a phone call – I had the job!

Serves: 8

INGREDIENTS:

½ recipe Chocolate Pastry (6)
½ recipe Vanilla Custard Filling (19)
6 figs, washed and dried
3 kiwi fruit, skinned and sliced
1 papaya
180 g/6 oz apple jelly for glaze

INSTRUCTIONS:

Press the pastry into eight 7.5 cm/ 3 in tins, prick the bases with a fork and bake at 180°C/360°F/ Gas 4 for 20 minutes. Remove from the tins to cool. Fill with the custard. Cut the figs into quarters and place three back to back on each tart centre to form a pyramid. Surround with half slices of kiwi fruit and small scoops of papaya cut with the melon baller. Melt the apple jelly in saucepan and brush on the fruit to glaze.

About keeping: Will keep for only a few hours after assembly.

Also try: Since fresh figs are often difficult to find or very expensive, top with any variety and many combinations of fresh or even poached, well-drained fruit.

Layered Chocolate Angel Food Cake

Chocolate angel food cake filled with layers of tangerine curd, iced with whipped *crème fraîche* and marble white chocolate shards.

EQUIPMENT:
Long thin bladed serrated knife
2 piping bags; 1 fitted with 5 cm, 2 in wide filling nozzle, the second with small leaf
Palette knife

When I first gave a recipe for lemon curd to my mother, she layered it into an angel food cake to serve at a church luncheon. There is an economy of means here; you get a striking, cloud-high layer cake without making three separate cakes. Also, citrus is an appropriate complement to this kind of cake. With vast quantities of vagrant egg whites in my life – a result of much custard making – I decided to reassess this American classic for myself. I had forgotten the endearing texture of angel food, and in testing this interpretation I reminded many others of its charm as well. With the icing treatment here it would make a wonderful birthday or special-occasion cake, served with a scoop of your favourite ice cream.

Serves: 12

INGREDIENTS:

1 recipe Chocolate Angel Food Cake (2)
1 recipe Tangerine Curd (22)
2 recipes Whipped Crème Fraîche *(26)*
1 recipe marble tinted white Chocolate Tiles (40B)

INSTRUCTIONS:

Slice the cake horizontally into three equal layers using a long serrated knife. Put the tangerine curd in the piping bag fitted with a filling nozzle and pipe half of it evenly on to the top of the first layer. Replace the second layer and repeat. Top with the third layer.

Spread the top and sides of cake with whipped *crème fraîche* using a palette knife. Break the chocolate tile into random shapes and stick it on to the covered surfaces.

With the second pastry bag fitted with a leaf nozzle pipe the remaining whipped *crème fraîche* back and forth between the tiles of chocolate all over the cake.

About keeping: Will keep for up to two days before icing in the refrigerator.

Also try: Fill the cake with Spiced Mascarpone (14) or Whiskey-Apricot Filling (15). Instead of icing it, try a simple drizzle of White or Dark Chocolate Ganache (23) or (24).

Chocolate-Hazelnut Tart

Chocolate pastry case with chocolate-hazelnut tart filling, decorated with a piped whipped cream bow.

EQUIPMENT:
Rolling pin
Pastry board (optional)
23 cm/9 in flan tin
Piping bag and 2.5 cm/1 in flat nozzle

Nut tarts have always seemed to me to be the dessert easiest to have too much of. The first great hazelnut pie I encountered was made by a one-time pastry chef at a favourite restaurant. When even scheduling my visits to coincide with this baker's weekly shift failed to deliver my quarry, I knew I had to create my own.

Serves: 8

INGREDIENTS:

$\frac{1}{2}$ *recipe Chocolate Pastry (6)*
1 recipe Chocolate-Hazelnut Tart Filling (21)
$\frac{1}{2}$ *recipe Whipped Cream (25)*

INSTRUCTIONS:

Roll out the pastry on lightly floured surface in to a circle. Place the pastry in the flan tin and trim off the excess pastry. Refrigerate the case for at least 15 minutes and pre-heat oven to 200°C/ 400°F/ Gas 6.

Pre-bake the case for 10 minutes. Fill the case with the hazelnut tart filling, and return it to the oven. Continue baking for 15 minutes, then reduce the temperature to 180°C/350°F/Gas 4 without opening door and bake for another 30 minutes, until edges of the filling begin to rise and the centre is set. Allow to cool before serving.

Pipe a whipped cream bow on each slice, as pictured, or simply dollop each plate with cream on the side.

About keeping: Serve fresh. Leftovers will keep for a couple of days.

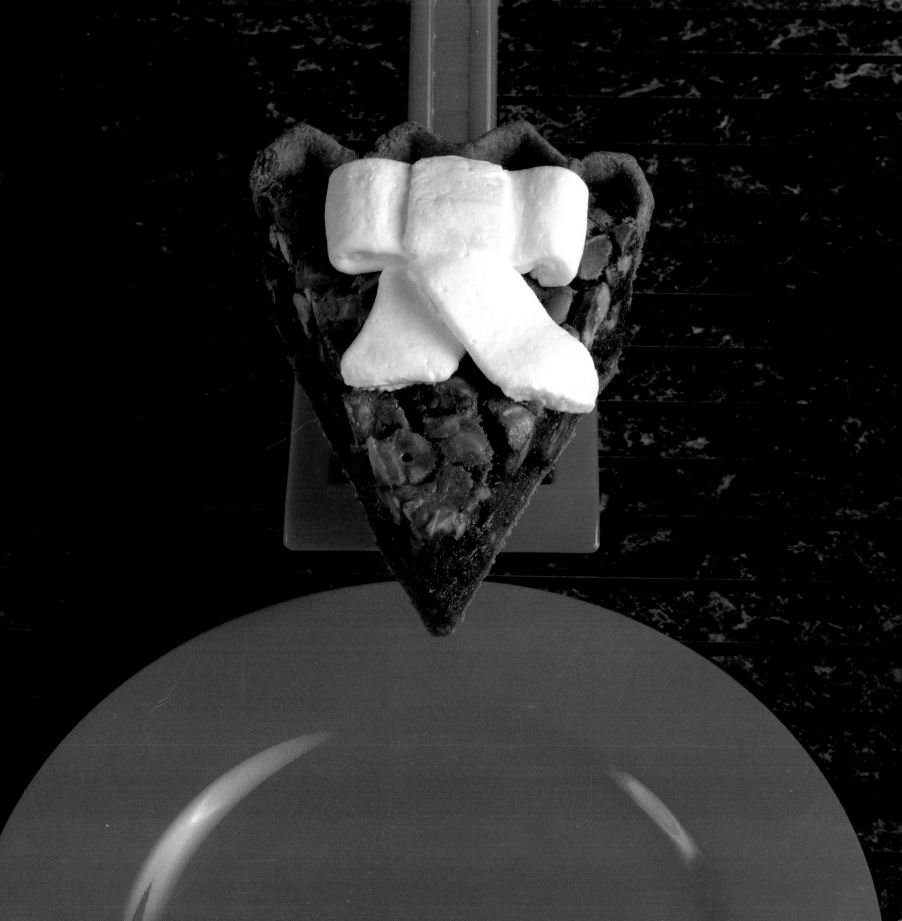

Poached Pears with Gold Leaves

Poached pear halves filled with spiced mascarpone in a pool of custard and bitter orange sauce, decorated with caramelized sugar lattice, gilded white chocolate leaves and spiced ground orange peel.

EQUIPMENT:
Scalpel
Cardboard for leaf
  template
Measuring jug or
  60 ml/2 fl oz ladle
Paring knife
Tablespoon or
  small ice cream
  scoop
Small, strong
  freezer bag

This elegant dessert evolved for a special birthday dinner for the owner of a luxury car dealership. Since he had recently completed construction of a sleek, beautifully designed sales and service centre, the dinner was served here at tables scattered among the gleaming Jaguars and Mercedes. All creamy pale and tawny gold, the dessert is a showy and complex display, yet its elements are simple and most can be made days ahead of serving.

Serves: 6

INGREDIENTS:

1 recipe gilded white Chocolate Tiles (40E)
1 recipe Vanilla Custard (31)
1 recipe Poached Pears (34)
1 recipe Spiced Mascarpone (14)
1 recipe Bitter Orange Sauce (28)
1 recipe Caramelized Sugar Lattice (44)
1 recipe Spiced Ground Orange Peel (41)

INSTRUCTIONS:

Cut a leaf shape from a piece of cardboard using a scalpel. Lay it on the gilded chocolate sheet and use the same blade to cut 12 leaf shapes from the chocolate.

Pour 60 ml/2 fl oz custard on to each of six dinner plates, tilting each to cover the base. Cut a small slice off the base of six pear halves so they won't roll about, and scoop 4 tablespoons of the mascarpone into each hollow. Set them in the sauce in the upper half of each plate.

Cut three of the best remaining pear halves in half again, and slice each half nearly through four times to fan; spread and lay on each plate to cover the lower rim of the plate.

Drizzle the bitter orange sauce from a strong freezer bag with a small hole cut in the corner into the custard round the pears.

Break the sheet of sugar lattice into pieces and press one into each scoop of mascarpone. Sprinkle some spiced orange peel over the whole plate, and lay a gilded chocolate leaf on either side of fanned out pear.

About keeping: Serve immediately once assembled.

Also try: This composition can be altered in perhaps more ways than any other included here - to range from dreamy to brightly coloured and playful. The pear can be filled with Vanilla Custard Filling (19), Chocolate Custard Filling (20), or Whipped *Crème Fraîche* (26). Raspberry Sauce (29) or Chocolate-Cognac Sauce (27) can be piped into the custard pool. The chocolate leaves can be replaced with any kind of white Chocolate Tiles (40), The sugar lattice can either be omitted or be replaced with Chocolate Filigree (42).

Layered Custard Cream Parfaits

Vanilla and chocolate custards folded into whipped cream and layered, with fresh raspberries; decorated with an array of whimsical accents.

EQUIPMENT:
Kitchen scales
3 large piping bags, one with large star nozzle
2 small bowls
Wire whisk
Rubber spatula
6 parfait or wine glasses

There is something intrinsically spectacular about layers of filling as seen through the side of a glass, and yet few effects are so easy to achieve. The challenge that caused the creation of this dessert was a major museum fund-raising event for 700 guests. While there was a need to match the special qualities of the institution with a really glamorous display, budget restrictions excluded the expensive ingredients and work-intensive nature of the most obvious choices. In this case, whipped cream was folded into a custard filling to lighten it, then combined with raspberries and a whimsical accent. The pre-filled rented glasses went to the party in their own crates, and in the end not one guest could resist the temptation of that last berry.

Serves: 6

INGREDIENTS:

$1\frac{1}{2}$ *recipes Whipped Cream (25)*
$\frac{1}{2}$ *recipe Vanilla Custard Filling (19)*
$\frac{1}{2}$ *recipe Chocolate Custard Filling (20)*
500 g/1 lb fresh raspberries
1 recipe any Chocolate Tiles (4), Caramelized Sugar Lattice (44), Chocolate Filigree (42) or Chocolate Decorations (43)

INSTRUCTIONS:

Reserve about 350 ml/12 fl oz of the whipped cream in a piping bag with the large star nozzle and refrigerate.

Scrape each custard into a small bowl; add 125 ml/4 fl oz whipped cream to each and whisk it in, smoothing the texture. Divide the remaining cream between the custards, then fold in gently with a rubber spatula.

Place a few berries in the bottom of each glass. Fill the two remaining piping bags with the two custard mixtures; pipe one layer of each alternately into the glasses, always against the glass first – in a ring, watching and turning the glass as you go – then filling in the centre of that layer. Top the glass with a layer more of berries, a coiled turban of piped whipped cream and your chosen decoration

About keeping: Will keep for one day covered, without whipped cream and decoration.

Also try: If you have a little more time and a steady hand, try piping a thin ring of Raspberry Sauce (29) against the glass between each layer of custard.

Joan Collins' Broken Heart

*Coeur à la crème
with a crack
that's lined in dark
chocolate tiles;
served with
raspberry sauce*

EQUIPMENT:
Double thickness
 of muslin to
 line mould
1 litre/1¾ pint
 heart-shaped mould
 with drainage holes
Scalpel
Large piping bag
 without nozzle
Wire rack on top of
 baking sheet
Small jug

I have loved the French dessert *coeur à la crème* from the time I first discovered it – the traditional heart-shaped mould and also the texture, best described as that of a cream cheese mousse. The process that produces it is unusual and interesting to observe but very simple. Cream and cottage cheeses are combined with whipped cream and used to fill a muslin-lined mould with holes in the base through which the whey in the cheese seeps out, firming the mixture inside. Thus the heart shape is a pun on the process – only the 'hearts' of the cheeses remain, as the name states.

Asked to create a dessert for a small buffet dinner for the cast of 'Dynasty', I made a broken heart, from whose dark-chocolate-sheathed break spills a blood-red raspberry sauce. I had just laid the heart's tray on the buffet as Joan Collins entered, spied it and caught her breath.

'Oh! Someone really made this?'

'Just for you, Joan,' I said from behind her as she turned and I presented myself.

'It's absolutely marvellous,' she enthused – as will you.

Serves: 4-6

NOTES:

This version is particularly well flavoured and doesn't really need fresh fruit, a customary accompaniment. The light, fluffy liqueured mousse is wonderful against the cold, crisp chocolate tiles and fruity raspberry sauce. If you don't have a regulation *coeur à la crème* mould punch holes in a heart-shaped tin you seldom use or make a temporary structure with foil shaped over cardboard.

INGREDIENTS:

1 recipe Coeur à la Crème Mixture (36)
½ recipe dark Chocolate Tiles (40)
1 recipe Raspberry Sauce (29)

INSTRUCTIONS:

Wet the muslin, squeeze out the excess moisture and line the mould.

Cut two strips of chocolate tile the same width as the depth of the mould, and about 5 cm/2 in longer than the diameter of the mould, using a scalpel. Cut both strips again into three unequal lengths and place them, in matching pairs, on top of each other.

Fill a piping bag with the *coeur à la crème* mixture. (A large paper clip will keep the filling from pouring through before you're ready.) Test standing the tiles in the mould to estimate where your heart will break, making sure to keep both them and your hands

cold. Remove the tiles, and pipe a small amount of the mixture in a line where the pairs of tiles will be. Push the tiles into the mixture so they will stand, their lengths flush. Pipe the remaining amount alternately on either side of crack, and fold the excess muslin over the filled mould. Place the mould on a wire rack over a baking sheet to drain, and refrigerate for at least 24 hours or up to two days.

To unmould, peel back the muslin from the surface, invert a plate over the top and turn both over. Remove the mould and muslin and slipping a knife into the crack between the pairs of tiles, slide the two halves apart to open the break. Pour the raspberry sauce into the break and pool it around the heart; serve more on the side in a small jug.

About keeping: Can be made for up to two days before serving.

Also try: Line crack with plain white Chocolate Tiles (40); serve with Bitter Orange Sauce (28), Apricot Sauce (30) or even Chocolate-Cognac Sauce (27).

Assorted Biscuits and Sweets

EQUIPMENT:
Kitchen scales
Small bowl over medium
 saucepan
Whisk
Baking parchment
 lined baking sheet

On a dessert buffet, packaged as gifts or just to munch on, these little sweets will please the eye as well as the palate. The techniques for producing them vary widely. Full recipes for three of those that are easiest to produce appear in the following pages (when component recipe number is indicated, refer to the index).

Baby Carrots in White Chocolate may seem strange but make more sense when you taste them; there's an allusion here to the classic American carrot cake with its sweet white icing, and the two textures offer a pleasing resonance of crispness. They were born as a decoration for a special cake I once did – a dacquoise covered in faux-wood-grained chocolate sheets to look like a cutting board, complete with grey chocolate knives with meringue handles. The event was a symposium on ritual and food attended by, of all people, Jesuits and psychologists. They were good enough together to survive their one-night stand. The carrots and chocolate, that is...

INGREDIENTS

250 g/8 oz white chocolate
1 bunch baby carrots (about 20)

INSTRUCTIONS:

Melt the chocolate in a small bowl over a saucepan a quarter full of simmering water. Whisk until smooth. Trim the carrot tops about 7.5 cm/3 in from the stem at a 45° angle, then wash the carrots (but don't scrub; leave skin intact to avoid carrot's moisture meeting chocolate) and dry thoroughly. Dip the carrots in the chocolate, raking the underside of each on the edge of the bowl as you remove it. Lay them on a baking parchment lined baking sheet until the chocolate is set.

Chocolate-Hazelnut Shortbread Squares contain the same filling found in the Chocolate-Hazelnut Tart, baked atop a chocolate version of classic Scottish shortbread.

INGREDIENTS:

1 recipe Chocolate Shortbread (9)
1 recipe Chocolate-Hazelnut Tart Filling (21)

INSTRUCTIONS:

Bake the pan of chocolate shortbread for 20 minutes at 180°C/350°F/Gas 4. While the shortbread is baking, make the tart filling.

Stir the hazelnut mixture well and pour over the shortbread, taking care to distribute the nuts evenly. Return to the oven and bake for another 30–35 minutes, until the topping is set. Cool and cut into 32 squares.

Crystallized Ginger in Plain Chocolate combines the tastes of ginger and chocolate that for many of my Jewish friends is a fond childhood memory. For those who've grown to love the zing of ginger this is the ultimate treatment.

EQUIPMENT:
Kitchen scales
Small bowl over medium saucepan
Whisk
Baking parchment lined baking sheet

INGREDIENTS

125 g/4 oz plain chocolate
90 g/3 oz crystallized ginger

INSTRUCTIONS:

Melt the chocolate in a small bowl over a small saucepan a quarter full of simmering water. Whisk until smooth.

Dip three quarters of each slice of ginger into the chocolate, then lay on a baking parchment lined baking sheet. Put in a cool, dry place to set.

Rich Hot Chocolate is a 'kids of all ages' pleaser that recollects the comforts of childhood, yet panders to an adult palate, with a creamy base and a hint of spice. It is substantial enough to be served in demitasse cups with a dessert buffet.

EQUIPMENT:
Kitchen scales
Can opener
Large saucepan
Measuring spoons
Wooden spoon
Whisk
Measuring jug

INGREDIENTS:

300 g/10 oz dark chocolate
350 ml/12 fl oz evaporated milk
1 tablespoon good quality instant coffee granules
1 stick cinnamon
840 ml/28 fl oz milk

INSTRUCTIONS:

Melt the chocolate in a small saucepan with the evaporated milk, instant coffee and cinnamon, stirring occasionally with a wooden spoon.

When the chocolate is melted, whisk the mixture until smooth. Whisk in the milk and heat through.

Pistachio Brittle on Chocolate (33) features the nuts often used as a decoration because of their unusual green colour. This presentation showcases their unique flavour.

Striped Refrigerator Biscuits (8) are a variation on the classic pin-wheel biscuits but they're actually easier to accurately form. The dough can be kept refrigerated for several weeks; you may wish to slice and bake a few at a time so they're always fresh.

Whiskey Prunes in Chocolate (32) will surprise many diners. Glazed with whiskey sugar and dipped in milk chocolate these prunes are truly wonderful.

About keeping: The biscuits will stay fresh for several days. Once sweets are dipped they should be served within a day to prevent problems with untempered chocolate (see Technique Notes). Carrots must be served soon after dipping to retain crispness; if necessary, they will last for 2 or 3 hours refrigerated. (Any bloom that develops in the refrigerator will not show on untinted white chocolate.) The hot chocolate will last for up to a week in the refrigerator.

Serves: Since the biscuit recipes yield 32 biscuits each, the sweets, including carrots, approximately 20 each, and the hot chocolate fills approximately 24 demitasse cups, this total buffet could serve between 20 and 30 guests.

The Component Recipes

Cakes

1 *Dark Chocolate Torte*

USE FOR:
Whiskey-Apricot
Chocolate Torte
Chocolate-
Chocolate Mousse
Torte

EQUIPMENT:
Kitchen scales
Large bowl over
large saucepan
Electric mixer and
bowl
Small bowl
Measuring jug and
spoons
Electric blender or
food processor
Whisk
Large rubber
spatula
25 cm/10 in spring-
form cake tin,
greased and lined
with baking
parchment

INGREDIENTS:

250g/8 oz dark chocolate
125g/4 oz unsalted butter
5 eggs
75 ml/2½ fl oz soured cream
1 tablespoon almond essence
60g/2 oz blanched almonds,
  toasted (see Technique Notes,
  page 10)
1 tablespoon soft plain flour
100g/3½ oz sugar

INSTRUCTIONS :

1 Melt the chocolate and butter together in a large bowl over a large saucepan a quarter full of simmering water. Pre-heat the oven to 180°C/350°F/Gas 4.

2 While the chocolate and butter are melting, separate the eggs: whites in the mixer bowl, yolks in a small bowl. Add the soured cream, vanilla essence and almond essence to the yolks and whisk until smooth.

3 Grind the nuts and flour finely together in a blender or food processor. When the chocolate is completely melted, whisk until smooth then remove from the heat. Whisk in the egg yolk mixture, then the nuts and flour.

4 Whisk the egg whites in the mixer at high speed. As the foam turns to fine bubbles, slowly shake the sugar into the bowl in a fine shower. Continue whisking until the whites are stiff and glossy but not dry.

5 Fold the egg whites one third at a time into the chocolate mixture with a large rubber spatula to make a smooth mixture.

6 Scrape the mixture into the prepared spring-form tin and bake for 40 minutes.

You may cool and cover the torte in the tin for further preparation at another time. Or, if continuing with an assembly using the torte, let it cool for 10 minutes, then remove the sides from the tin base to cool the torte completely.

About keeping: The torte will keep, frozen, for several months.

Makes: One 25 cm/10 in torte

Chocolate Angel Food Cake

2

60 g/2 oz soft plain flour
45 g/1½ oz cocoa
300 g/10 oz sugar
12 egg whites
1½ teaspoons cream of tartar
¼ teaspoon salt
2 teaspoons vanilla essence
2 teaspoons chocolate essence
½ teaspoon almond essence

INSTRUCTIONS:

1 Pre-heat the oven to 190°C/
375°F/Gas 5. Sift together the flour,
cocoa and 150 g/5 oz of the sugar.
Set aside.

2 Add the cream of tartar and salt to
the egg whites in a mixer bowl.
Whisk until fine bubbles begin to
form, then whisking continuously,
slowly shake into the egg whites the
remaining 150 g/5 oz sugar, in a fine
steady shower. Whisk to the stiff
peak stage.

3 Scoop this meringue into a large
bowl and gently fold in the vanilla,
chocolate and almond essences.
Then, disturbing the meringue as
little as necessary, fold in the flour
mixture one third at a time.

4 Transfer the mixture to the mould
by scoops with a rubber spatula,
taking care not to leave any air
pockets. Bake for 30 minutes, until
the cake is set and springy. Invert on
to a wire rack to cool, and cool
completely before sliding a knife
between pan and cake to remove it.

About keeping: Covered (but not
necessarily refrigerated), the cake
will keep for several days.

Makes: One 25 cm/10 in cake

USE FOR:
Layered Chocolate
Angel Food Cake

EQUIPMENT:
Kitchen scales
Sieve
Electric mixer and
bowl
Measuring spoons
Large bowl
Large rubber
spatula
25 cm/10 in metal
ring mould, about
10 cm/4 in deep,
greased
Wire rack
Thin bladed knife

3 *Chocolate Génoise*

USE FOR:
Chocolate Ribbon
Cake

EQUIPMENT:
Kitchen scales
Medium saucepan
Sieve
Baking parchment
Electric mixer
 and bowl
Whisk
Slotted wooden
 spatula
Small saucepan
Measuring spoons
Large rubber
 spatula
Large bowl
 30 x 42.5 x 2.5
 cm/12 x 17 x 1 in
Swiss roll tin,
 greased and lined
 with baking
 parchment
Wooden cocktail
 stick
Wire rack

NOTES:

Every confection made from an egg leavened mixture is a race against the collapse of air bubbles: a race against time. This is specially true of *génoise*. While there are few ingredients and they are combined in a few simple steps, easy success demands a deft flow of well-orchestrated moves without interruption. In other words, don't answer the phone. Several thousand batches ago they all laughed at my rubber-bottomed *génoise*, but this versatile cake soon became one of the fundamentals of my career. These instructions describe as accurately as possible what I've learned.

INGREDIENTS:

90 g/3 oz soft plain flour
22 g/¾ oz cocoa
200 g/7 oz sugar
6 eggs
60 g/2 oz unsalted butter
2 teaspoons vanilla essence
½ teaspoon almond essence

INSTRUCTIONS:

1 Pre-heat the oven to 180°C/350°F/Gas 4. Heat about 5 cm/2 in water in a medium saucepan over medium heat. (Make sure your mixer's bowl will fit over it stably, well above the water.)

2 Sift the flour and cocoa together on to the baking parchment. Weigh the sugar and have it ready beside the mixer.

3 Break the eggs into the mixer bowl and whisk to combine. Place the bowl over the boiling water in the saucepan and stir briskly and constantly with a slotted wooden spatula until the eggs are hot but not curdled. Remove the bowl from the saucepan and immediately add the sugar and begin whisking with the mixer at high speed.

4 Remove the saucepan of water from the heat. Reduce the heat to low and set the butter in the small saucepan over it to melt. As the eggs expand with whisking add the vanilla and almond essences. When they have reached maximum volume the mixture will stop moving up the sides of the bowl and, when the beater is lifted, the mixture will not run from the tines but fall in a ribbon.

5 Scrape the mixture into a large bowl with a spatula. Shake half the flour-cocoa mixture from the parchment over the cake mixture and fold in carefully, turning the bowl and scraping the sides. Fold in the other half. Pour the butter over the mixture and fold that in.

6 Scrape the mixture into the prepared tin and bake for 15–20 minutes, until a wooden cocktail stick comes out clean and the cake begins to pull away from edges of the tin. Set on a wire rack to cool. If not using immediately, the cake can be wrapped in the tin for later assembly.

About keeping: Will keep for several days wrapped and refrigerated; a one day rest will actually make the cake easier to work with when assembling a dessert. It can also be frozen successfully for several weeks.

Makes: One 30 x 42.5 cm/12 x 17 in cake

Chocolate Custard Cake

4

INGREDIENTS:

90 g/3½ oz cocoa
180 ml/6 fl oz water
2 tablespoons tequila
60 g/2 oz unsalted butter
100 g/3½ oz sugar
3 eggs
*60 g/2 oz blanched almonds,
  toasted and ground (see Technique
  Notes, page 10)*
*½ teaspoon Spiced Ground Orange
  Peel (41)*
2 egg whites

INSTRUCTIONS:

1 Pre-heat the oven to 180°C/ 350°F/Gas 4. Whisk the cocoa, water and tequila in a small bowl until smooth.

2 Cream the butter and sugar together in a food processor until light and fluffy. Scrape the mixture into the bowl of an electric mixer and whisk in the three eggs, then the cocoa mixture. Scrape into a large bowl and fold in the nuts and peel.

3 Clean and dry the mixer bowl and beaters for the egg whites. Beat them until stiff but not dry, then fold into the cake mixture. Pour into the greased loaf tin and bake for 30 minutes. The cake will be baked about 2.5 cm/1 in from the surface but still very soft and gooey in the centre; the wooden cocktail stick test for doneness will not work here. Cool to just slightly warm before running a knife round the edges and turning out to slice. Do not turn out on a wire rack - since this cake is quite soft it might fall between the wires.

About keeping: This cake is best eaten soon after baking, but it will still be excellent several days later (although its texture will be more homogenous).

Makes: One 23 x 13 cm/9 x 5 in loaf cake; ten 2-2.5 cm/¾-1 in slices

USE FOR:
Mexican Chocolate
Custard Cake

EQUIPMENT:
Kitchen scales
Small bowl
Measuring jug
Measuring spoons
Whisk
Food processor
Rubber spatula
Electric mixer
and bowl
Large bowl
1 litre/1¾ pint loaf
tin, greased
Thin bladed knife

Pastries

5 *Almond-Hazelnut Meringue*

USE FOR:

Lightning Bolt
  Dacquoise
Meringue and
  Chocolate
  Chequerboard

EQUIPMENT:

Kitchen scales
Wide pastry brush
30 x 42.5 x 2.5 cm
  12 x 17 x 7 in Swiss
  roll tin
Baking parchment
Food processor
Electric mixer and
  bowl
Large bowl
Large rubber spatula

NOTES:

This crispy, nutty sheet of meringue is my favourite building material, since it can easily be cut into shapes and provides a rigid base for exotic decoration. I have used it for everything from a leaping rainbow trout for the 85th birthday of an avid fly fisherman to an edible reproduction of the Golden Gate Bridge, 1.8 m/6 ft long, complete with chocolate cars, for a bank reception. In this book it makes two appearances - as the heart of the Lightning Bolt Dacquoise (16) and the base of the Meringue and Chocolate Chequerboard buffet (32) display.

INGREDIENTS:

2 tablespoons butter, melted
250 g/8 oz blanched almonds, toasted (see Technique Notes)
125 g/4 oz hazelnuts, toasted and rubbed to remove skins (see Technique Notes)
40g/1¼ oz unbleached plain flour
350 g/12 oz sugar
8 egg whites (freeze yolks or just refrigerate them to reserve for another use)

INSTRUCTIONS:

1 Pre-heat the oven to 200°C/400°F/Gas 6. Brush the Swiss roll tin with the melted butter, then line it with baking parchment and brush again.

2 Combine both kinds of nuts, the flour and 900 g/10 oz of the sugar: in a food processor and process until the mixture resembles coarse crumbs.

3 Whisk the egg whites at high speed until the soft peak stage, then slowly and gently shake in the remaining sugar. Continue whisking to the stiff peak stage.

4 Scrape the egg whites into a large bowl with a rubber spatula then fold in the nut mixture one third at a time. Scrape into the prepared tin and use the spatula to spread 1 cm/¼ in deep as evenly as possible.

5 Bake for 25 minutes until the top is browned and the meringue pulls away from sides of the tin and feels firm to the touch. Cool for 10 minutes, then turn out on to another sheet of baking parchment and peel the paper off the meringue. Set aside to cool completely before continuing.

About keeping: Once cool, the meringue may be cut, wrapped and stored for a few days or even frozen before you assemble your presentation.

Makes: One 30 x 42.5 cm/12 x 17 in meringue

Chocolate Pastry

6

INGREDIENTS:

275 g/9 oz unbleached plain flour
3 tablespoons cocoa
3 tablespoons sugar
125 g/4 oz unsalted butter, chilled
60 g/2 oz lard
75 ml/2½ fl oz cold water

INSTRUCTIONS:

1 Sift the flour, cocoa and sugar together into a food processor. Cut the butter into chunks, then add to the flour mixture with the lard and process until the mixture resembles breadcrumbs.

2 Add the cold water and process until the pastry begins to form a ball. Form the pastry into 2 equal flat circles. Wrap and refrigerate for at least 30 minutes, to allow the gluten in the flour to relax.

About keeping: You can freeze the pastry for up to two weeks.

Makes: Enough pastry for two 23 cm/9 in tart cases, one 23 cm/9 in two-crust pie, or sixteen 7.5 cm/3 in tartlet cases

USE FOR:
Chocolate-Hazelnut Tart Chocolate Pastry
Latticed Apricot Tart
The Tomlin Tarts

EQUIPMENT
Kitchen scales
Measuring jug and spoons
Sieve
Food processor
Cling film

Chocolate Sandwich Biscuits

INGREDIENTS:

200 g/7 oz sugar
180 g/6 oz unsalted butter
2 eggs
1 teaspoon vanilla essence
275 g/9 oz unbleached plain flour
30 g/1 oz cocoa
¾ teaspoon bicarbonate of soda
¼ teaspoon salt

INSTRUCTIONS:

1 Pre-heat the oven to 180°C/350°F/Gas 4. Cream the sugar and butter together in a food processor, then add the eggs, and vanilla essence and process until smooth.

2 Scrape the mixture into a medium bowl. Sift together the flour, cocoa, bicarbonate of soda and salt. Work the dry ingredients into the butter-egg mixture with a wooden spatula until it forms a solid mass. Shape the dough into a flat square.

3 Roll out the lightly floured dough on a lightly floured surface to 35.5 cm/14 in square and 5 mm/¼ in thick. With a ruler and paring knife, cut the dough into 16 7.5 cm/3 in squares (four up and four across). Slide them on to ungreased baking sheets with a palette knife.

4 Bake for 10 minutes. Remove to a wire rack with a palette knife. The biscuits must be completely cooled before using.

About keeping: Wrap the biscuits if you are not using them right away, so they'll remain moist and cake-like when paired with the ice cream.

Makes: Sixteen 7.5 cm/3 in biscuits (for eight ice cream sandwiches)

USE FOR:
Chocolate Chip-Mint
Ice Cream Sandwiches

EQUIPMENT:
Kitchen scales
Food processor
Measuring spoons
Medium bowl
Sieve
Wooden spatula
Rolling pin
Pastry board (optional)
Ruler
Paring knife
Palette knife
Baking sheets
Wire rack

8 *Striped Refrigerator Biscuits*

USE FOR:
Assorted Biscuits and
 Sweets

EQUIPMENT:
Kitchen scales
Food processor
Measuring spoons
Medium bowl
Wooden spatula
Cling film
Pastry board
 (optional)
Rolling pin
Ruler
Paring knife
Baking sheets
Palette knife
Whisk
Pastry brush
Wire rack

NOTES:

Unsweetened chocolate is not widely available in Britain. Bittersweet chocolate is the closest substitute, although it is sweetened.

INGREDIENTS:

250 g/8 oz unsalted butter
150 g/5 oz sugar
1 egg yolk
1 teaspoon vanilla essence
¼ teaspoon almond essence
350 g/12 oz unbleached plain flour
*60 g/2 oz unsweetened or
 bittersweet chocolate, melted and
 cooled*

INSTRUCTIONS:

1 Cream the butter and sugar together in a food processor. Add the egg yolk and vanilla essence and process again until smooth.

2 Measure half - about 180 ml/6 fl oz of this mixture into a medium bowl. Add the almond essence, then 170 g/5¾ oz of the flour. Stir them in with a wooden spoon, then work the dough with your hands into a flat, square mass. Wrap in cling film and refrigerate.

3 Put the second half of the butter mixture in a bowl and whisk in the chocolate. Add the remaining flour and stir in with a wooden spatula, then work the dough with your hands to form a flat rectangle. Wrap and refrigerate.

4 Roll out the vanilla half of the dough into a 23 cm/9 in square 1 cm/¼ in thick on a lightly floured surface. Trim the top edge with a ruler and knife, then slice into four 5cm/2 in strips 23 cm/9 in long. Transfer to the back of a baking sheet with a long palette knife. (If strips stick to surface, put a little flour on tip of the palette knife.

5 Roll out the chocolate half of the dough on a lightly floured surface to a 23 x 28 cm/9 x 11 in rectangle about 1 cm/¼ in thick. Trim the narrow edge with a knife and ruler, then slice the rest into five 23 x 5 cm/9 x 2 in strips.

6 Brush the surface of the chocolate strip closest to you with water. Using a palette knife lift one of the vanilla strips and place on top of a chocolate strip. Repeat, alternating colours and brushing with water between each layer; finish with the last chocolate strip. Press down to seal the layers.

7 Wrap the completed log of layered dough tightly in cling film and refrigerate for several hours. To bake, pre-heat the oven to 180°C/350°F/ Gas 4. Cut the dough into 1 cm/¼ in slices and lay on an ungreased baking sheet. Bake for 10–15 minutes. If some layers separate, place them together on the baking sheet and they will join while baking. Carefully transfer to a wire rack to cool.

About keeping: The baked biscuits will keep well, but if you don't need them all at once bake only as many as you want; keep the remainder of the dough, refrigerated, for as long as 2–3 weeks.

Makes: About 32 biscuits

Chocolate Shortbread

INGREDIENTS:

275 g/9 oz unbleached plain flour
22 g/¾ oz cocoa
80 g/2⅔ oz icing sugar
250 g/8 oz unsalted butter

INSTRUCTIONS:

1 Pre-heat the oven to 180°C/350°F/Gas 4. Sift the flour, cocoa and sugar together into a food processor.

2 Cut the butter into 15 g/½ oz pieces and add to the flour mixture. Process until the butter is just cut in and the mixture looks like coarse crumbs. Do not overprocess.

3 Place the mixture in the baking tin,

then smooth to an even layer and press in with your fingers. Bake for 20 minutes. If making plain shortbread, remember to cut it into squares before it cools. If making Chocolate-Hazelnut Shortbread Squares, continue with the directions under Assorted Biscuits and Sweets.

About keeping: Shortbread will keep for several weeks; in fact, the flavour improves as the butter ages a bit.

Makes: 32 squares

USE FOR:
Chocolate-Hazelnut
Shortbread Squares
(Assorted Biscuits
and Sweets)

EQUIPMENT:
Kitchen scales
Sieve
Food processor
23 x 33 x 5 cm/
9 x 13 x 2 in
baking tin, greased

Chocolate Tortellini

10

INGREDIENTS:

135 g/4½ oz plain flour
3 tablespoons cocoa
3 tablespoons icing sugar
1 egg
2 tablespoons water
1 tablespoon chocolate essence
100 g/3½ oz sweetened chestnut
  purée
75 g/2½ oz ricotta cheese
30 g/1 oz blanched almonds,
  toasted and ground (see Technique
  Notes, page 10)
1 egg yolk

INSTRUCTIONS:

1 Place the flour, cocoa and sugar in a food processor; process until well combined.

2 Add the egg, water and chocolate essence and process until the mixture forms a ball. With floured hands remove the dough and form it into a flat square. Wrap it in cling film and refrigerate for at least 30 minutes.

3 Blend the chestnut purée, ricotta cheese, almonds and egg yolk together in a small bowl. Set aside.

4 Roll out the dough on a lightly floured surface into an 8 cm/20 in square. Cut 36 rounds of pasta with a biscuit cutter. Pull background scraps away and discard.

5 Place 1 teaspoon of the filling on each round. Spray the surfaces with a mist of water, then fold each in half and pinch the edges to seal. Pull the two points towards each other across the back fold, and pinch together. Repeat with all 36, transferring each to a wire rack as completed. Freeze.

6 When ready to serve, drop the tortellini into a large pan of rapidly boiling water and cook for 3-5 minutes or until *al dente*.

About keeping: Open-freeze the tortellini, then bag and store until ready to use (or the moisture in the cheese will migrate into the pasta and ruin it). They will keep 2-3 weeks frozen and, once cooked, only minutes.

Makes: 36 tortellini

USE FOR:
Chocolate Tortellini
in Pear Syrup

EQUIPMENT:
Kitchen scales
Measuring spoons
Food processor
Small bowl
Pastry board
(optional)
Rolling pin
6 cm/2½ in
biscuit cutter
Spray bottle
Wire rack
Large saucepan

11 *Chocolate Chip Eclairs*

USE FOR:
Custard-filled
 Chocolate Chip
 Eclairs

EQUIPMENT:
Kitchen scales
Small bowl
Whisk
Measuring jug
Heavy-based
 medium saucepan
Wooden spoon
Electric mixer and
 bowl
Rubber spatula
Piping bag with
 large star nozzle
Chilled buttered
 baking sheet
Wire rack

NOTES:

Make a double batch of these and freeze some – they reheat well and are excellent with many other fillings. Keep the chocolate chips small, or they will make holes in the surface of the pastry when they melt (and allow air to escape and deflate the puffing).

INGREDIENTS:

2 eggs, beaten
60 g/2 oz unsalted butter
125 ml/4 fl oz water
70 g/2⅓ oz unbleached plain flour
1 tablespoon finely chopped dark
 chocolate

INSTRUCTIONS:

1 Break the eggs into a small bowl and whisk slightly to combine.

2 Bring the butter and water to the boil in a medium saucepan over a medium-high heat, then add the flour and beat vigorously with a wooden spoon until the mixture forms a ball and comes away from the sides of the pan.

3 Place the pastry in a mixer bowl and begin beating at medium speed, adding the eggs in a stream. Continue beating after the eggs are incorporated until the texture changes from sloppy to smooth, thick and sticky. Scrape the mixture into the egg bowl, cover and refrigerate for 1 hour or until cold enough for it not to melt the chocolate. If you plan to continue, pre-heat the oven to 200°C/400°F/Gas 6, but the mixture will keep for up to a day at this point.

4 Fold the chopped chocolate into the cold mixture. Fill a piping bag fitted with a large star nozzle with the mixture and pipe out six 13 cm/5 in long eclairs on to a cold, buttered baking sheet, turning the bag as you pipe to create a spiral effect. (If the baking sheet isn't cold the butter will be slippery, and the mixture will slide away from you as you pipe and you will lose control of the shape.)

5 Bake for 30 minutes or until golden brown. Slice open lengthways to allow excess moisture to escape. Cool on a wire rack.

About keeping: What you have to defeat here is the migration of moisture from the interior to what you wish to remain a crisp exterior. Therefore, if serving in a few hours leave uncovered; if keeping for a day or longer freeze and re-crisp in a 200°C/400°F/Gas 6 oven for about 10 minutes before serving.

Makes: 6 eclairs

Chocolate Pancakes

NOTES:

It is so easy to make pancakes once you're set up for it, and because they freeze so well, I recommend you make more than you need and store the rest for another time and another filling. Be forewarned: the first one never works. If it sticks, clean the pan thoroughly and be sure the pan is back up to temperature before trying again.

INGREDIENTS:

135 g/4½ oz unbleached plain flour
22 g/¾ oz cocoa
50 g/1⅔ oz sugar
3 eggs
1 teaspoon vanilla essence
1 teaspoon chocolate essence
350 ml/12 fl oz milk
Butter for frying

INSTRUCTIONS:

1 Combine the flour, cocoa, sugar, eggs, vanilla and chocolate essence in a blender or food processor, then add the milk in a stream while the machine is running. Refrigerate for 2 hours or overnight before making the pancakes.

2 To cook, heat the crêpe pan to medium high and wipe with a wad of kitchen paper smeared in butter. Pour about 45 ml/1½ fl oz batter into the pan using a small ladle, immediately tilting the pan to cover the base with the thinnest possible sheet of batter. Adjust the amount you pour according to the amount required to just cover.

3 Cook for 1½-2 minutes on the first side, until browned. Turn the pancake over and cook for 1 minute more and turn out. Repeat, occasionally wiping the pan with more of the butter, using only enough to keep the pancakes from sticking. Stack the completed pancakes with strips of greaseproof paper between them. Wrap and refrigerate until you fill them.

About keeping: Refrigerated, the batter keeps for two days; cooked pancakes for one week. Frozen pancakes keep for several months.

Makes: 18–20 pancakes

USE FOR:
Chocolate Pancakes with Flambéed Oranges

EQUIPMENT:
Kitchen scales
Measuring jug and spoons
Electric blender or food processor
15 cm/6 in crêpe pan
Small ladle
Greaseproof paper strips to separate pancakes

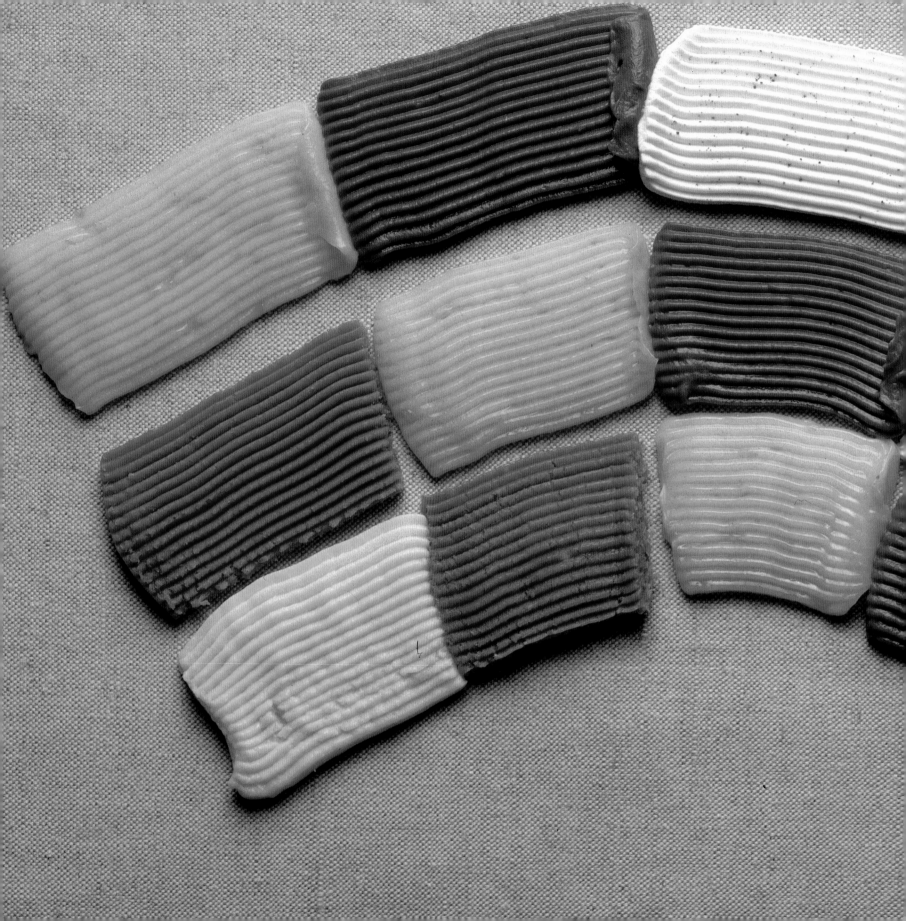

Fillings & Icings

13 *Dark Chocolate Mousse*

USE FOR:
Chocolate-Chocolate
  Mousse Torte
Meringue and
  Chocolate
  Chequerboard

EQUIPMENT:
Kitchen scales
Medium bowl over
  medium saucepan
Knife
Electric mixer and
  bowl
Small bowl
Whisk
Measuring spoons
Large bowl
Large rubber
  spatula
Measuring jug

NOTES:

The keys to success here are the gradual cooling of the chocolate as various ingredients are added, the texture of the egg whites and your folding technique; if the whites are too stiff you will tend to over-fold to incorporate them. If necessary, live with a few flecks of white rather than risk loss of volume.

INGREDIENTS:

500 g/1 lb dark chocolate
250 g/8 oz unsalted butter
8 eggs
2 tablespoons sugar
125 ml/4 fl oz double cream

INSTRUCTIONS:

1 Melt the chocolate in a medium bowl over a medium saucepan a quarter full of simmering water.

2 While the chocolate is melting, cut the butter into small chunks and separate the eggs: whites in the mixer bowl, yolks in a small bowl.

3 Whisk the chocolate until smooth. Remove the bowl and saucepan from the heat, add the butter and whisk until all the lumps are melted.

4 Remove the bowl from the saucepan and whisk in the egg yolks until smooth.

5 Use the mixer to whisk the egg whites, adding the sugar slowly as they reach the soft peak stage. Stop when they are stiff but not dry.

6 Scrape the chocolate mixture into a large bowl, then fold in the egg whites a third at a time.

7 Whip the cream until stiff, then fold into the mousse. Refrigerate: about 2 hours to use as torte filling or at least 4 hours to set (best set overnight).

About keeping: Will keep for up to one week in the refrigerator.

Makes: 8 servings

Spiced Mascarpone

14

INGREDIENTS:

350 g/12 oz mascarpone cheese
1 tablespoon finely chopped
  crystallized ginger
1 tablespoon clear honey
2 teaspoons Frangelico liqueur
¼ teaspoon spiced Ground Orange
  Peel (41)
½ teaspoon ground cinnamon
¼ teaspoon grated nutmeg
¼ teaspoon ground cloves

INSTRUCTIONS:

1 Put all the ingredients into a bowl and fold together with a rubber spatula.

2 Refrigerate to re-firm the cheese: it will thin considerably as you work it. But don't worry - it will scoop.

About keeping: Will keep for up to one week.

Makes: 350 g/12 oz spiced mascarpone

USE FOR:
Chocolate Pancakes with
Flambéed Oranges
Chocolate Ribbon Cake
Layered Chocolate
Angel Food Cake
Meringue and Chocolate
Chequerboard
Poached Pears with
Gold leaves

EQUIPMENT:
Kitchen scales
Measuring spoons
Medium bowl
Rubber spatula

Whiskey-Apricot Filling

INGREDIENTS:

150 ml/5 fl oz bourbon whiskey
250 g/8 oz dried apricots
50 g/1⅓ oz sugar
60 ml/2 fl oz water

INSTRUCTIONS:

1 Combine the whiskey and dried apricots in a food processor and blend until roughly chopped: it will be a bumpy process.

2 Scrape the fruit into a saucepan, add the sugar and water and bring to the boil over medium-high heat. Reduce to low and simmer for 5 minutes, stirring occasionally but avoiding the fumes. (They can be intoxicating in the literal sense.)

3 Cover the pan, remove from the heat and do not disturb until completely cooled. Scrape into a storage container and chill until ready to serve.

About keeping: Will keep for several months in the refrigerator.

Makes: 350 ml/12 fl oz filling

USE FOR:
Chocolate Chip-Mint Ice
Cream Sandwiches
Chocolate-Chocolate
Mousse Torte
Layered Chocolate
Angel Food Cake
Whiskey-Apricot
Chocolate Torte

EQUIPMENT:
Kitchen scales
Measuring jug
Food processor
Rubber spatula
Medium saucepan
with lid
Spoon

16 *Coffee Buttercream*

EQUIPMENT-
Kitchen scales
Electric mixer
 with bowl and
 paddle attachment
Measuring spoons
Rubber spatula
Sieve

NOTES:

This is the only kind of buttercream I can bear, the bitter coffee cutting the high sugar-fat content. I recall once early in my career making a bride-to-be cry when I said raspberry buttercream icing would make her guests gag and they'd all want coffee instead of champagne. I've learned a little about client relations since then, though I've still managed to avoid making an oversweet buttercream wedding cake. And whenever I do use buttercream, I put the coffee in it myself.

INGREDIENTS:

350 g/12 oz unsalted butter,
 softened
2 tablespoons double cream
2 tablespoons good-quality instant
 coffee granules
1 teaspoon water
2 egg yolks
250 g/8 oz icing sugar

INSTRUCTIONS:

1 Beat the softened butter in a mixer until smooth, using a paddle-shaped attachment if possible, then beat in the cream.

2 Dissolve the instant coffee in the water. Add the coffee and egg yolks to the butter and beat until well mixed, scraping the sides of the bowl.

3 Sift the icing sugar, then add half at a time to the butter mixture, combining at low speed first to avoid a sugar-coated kitchen. Finish at high speed, beating until smooth. Cover with cling film and refrigerate if you don't plan to use it right away, but remember you will have to return it to room temperature before you can work with it again.

About keeping: Can either be kept refrigerated for one week or be frozen.

Makes: About 500 g/1 lb buttercream

Apricot Tart Filling

INGREDIENTS:

4 x 425 g/14 oz cans stoned apricots in heavy syrup
2 tablespoons brandy
2 tablespoons cornflour
100 g/3½ oz sugar
¼ teaspoon almond essence

INSTRUCTIONS:

1 Drain the fruit into a large sieve over a medium bowl.

2 Measure 150 ml/5 fl oz of the drained syrup into a medium saucepan. Discard the remaining syrup and transfer the apricots to a bowl.

3 Combine the brandy and cornflour and whisk until smooth, then scrape into the saucepan. Stir in the sugar and almond essence and bring to the boil over medium heat and boil for 1 minute. Stir the thickened syrup into the fruit, then cool before filling a tart so you don't melt the pastry!

About keeping: Can be made up to a week before making the tart and kept in the refrigerator.

Makes: Enough to fill a 23 cm/9 in tart

USE FOR:
Chocolate Pastry
Latticed Apricot Tart

EQUIPMENT:
Kitchen scales
Can opener
Large sieve
Medium bowl
Medium saucepan
Measuring spoons
Small whisk
Rubber spatula

Flambéed Oranges

18

INGREDIENTS:

6–8 oranges, preferably large, meaty, deeply coloured navels or Valencias – to equal 540 g/18 oz pulp after preparation
300 ml/10 fl oz Grand Marnier
70 g/2⅓ oz sugar

INSTRUCTIONS:

1 Cut off both ends of each orange to the flesh and peel. Cut each orange in half lengthways, then cut a deep 'V' inside each half to remove the core and thick area of membrane where the sections meet. Push out any pips. Place each half flat side down and cut into thirds lengthways and then across in 1 cm/½ in slices.

2 Heat the Grand Marnier in a sauté pan over medium-high heat, then ignite it with a match and add the orange slices at once. Shake the pan to mix and burn off all the alcohol. When the flames die down and the oranges are heated through transfer them to a storage container using a slotted spoon.

3 Add the sugar to the Grand Marnier, stir and reduce to a thick syrup. Pour the sauce over the oranges. Serve in pancakes.

About keeping: Can be refrigerated for up to two days (serve at room temperature).

Makes: About 540 g/18 oz; enough to fill 12 pancakes

USE FOR:
Chocolate Pancakes
with Flambéed
Oranges

EQUIPMENT:
Kitchen scales
Sharp paring knife
Measuring jug
Large sauté pan
Slotted metal spoon

19 *Vanilla Custard Filling*

USE FOR:
Chocolate Ribbon
 Cake
Custard-filled
 Chocolate
 Chip Eclairs
Layered Custard
 Cream Parfaits
Meringue and
 Chocolate
 Chequerboard
Poached Pears with
 Gold Leaves
The Tomlin Tarts

EQUIPMENT:
Kitchen scales
Measuring jug
Sieve
2 medium bowls
Whisk
Measuring spoons
Heavy-based large
 saucepan
Rubber spatula
Slotted wooden
 spatula
Cling film

NOTES:

This custard filling is a well-flavoured, thick-textured building material with many uses. It will support layered cakes without slipping and fill pastry cases with less "sogging" than do the alternatives. If you're left with a few lumps when the cooking has finished pick them out or live with them - do not attempt to sieve this after cooking or you will break the combination of the molecules and it won't be as firm. Also, be sure to use soft plain flour, which is more finely milled.

The one time I thought these things wouldn't matter I ended up at a party wiping blobs of filling from the sides of a cake that had disgorged half its contents on a tide of slippery custard. Even the dozen skewers with which I had impaled the cake had failed to staunch the flow of disaster, with 30 minutes left before the arrival of the guests. I simply cleaned the ooze, straightened the tilt, re-piped the sides and covered the top with flowers. (This is the only delivery problem I have ever had, and you are sworn to secrecy.) They thanked me later for a delicious cake, but I didn't take another private commission for 6 months!

INGREDIENTS:

40 g/1⅓ oz plus 1 tablespoon soft
 plain flour
150 g/5 oz sugar
500 ml/16 fl oz milk
6 egg yolks
2 teaspoons vanilla essence
¼ teaspoon almond essence

INSTRUCTIONS:

1 Sift the flour into the sugar in a medium bowl, and whisk together until completely combined.

2 Whisk 125 ml/4 fl oz of the milk into the egg yolks in another medium bowl. Then whisk that mixture into the flour-sugar mixture until it is completely smooth and the sugar is dissolved. Whisk in the vanilla and almond essences.

3 Heat the remaining milk in a heavy-based saucepan over a medium-high heat. Just as the milk boils, whisk half of it into the egg-flour mixture, then scrape all of that back into the pan.

4 Immediately begin stirring with a slotted wooden spatula and stir constantly until the custard mixture begins to thicken. The price of not using a double boiler is eternal vigilance.

5 As the custard thickens it will go through a lumpy stage. Don't be alarmed, but pick up the speed of your stirring and beat the custard with a slotted spatula – and use an oven glove since the mixture can spatter and will be hot. Continue to beat and it will smooth out and

thicken just before boiling. Stir and boil for 1 minute.

6 Immediately remove the pan from the heat and transfer the custard to a storage container, covering the surface with cling film to prevent a skin from forming. Cool before refrigerating. It can be used as soon as it is cold.

About keeping: Will keep for up to one week in the refrigerator.

Makes: About 750 ml/1¼ pints custard

Chocolate Custard Filling

INGREDIENTS:

40 g/1⅓ oz soft plain flour
22 g/¾ oz cocoa
150 g/5 oz sugar
500 ml/16 fl oz milk
6 egg yolks
2 teaspoons vanilla essence
¼ teaspoon almond essence
½ teaspoon chocolate essence

INSTRUCTIONS:

1 Sift the flour and cocoa into the sugar in a medium bowl, and whisk together until completely combined.

2 In another medium bowl, whisk 125 ml/4 fl oz of the milk into the egg yolks. Then whisk that mixture into the flour-sugar mixture until it is completely smooth and the sugar is dissolved. Whisk in the vanilla, almond and chocolate essences.

3 Heat the remaining milk in a heavy-based saucepan over a medium high heat. Just as the milk boils, whisk half of it into the egg-flour mixture, then scrape all of that back into the pan.

4 Immediately begin stirring with a slotted wooden spatula and stir constantly until the custard mixture begins to thicken.

5 As the custard mixture thickens it will go through a lumpy stage. Don't be alarmed, but increase the speed of your stirring and beat the custard with the slotted spatula and use an oven glove since the mixture can spatter and will be hot. Continue to beat, and it will smooth out and thicken just before boiling. Stir and boil for 1 minute.

6 Immediately remove the pan from the heat and scrape the custard filling into a storage container, covering the surface with cling film to prevent a skin from forming. Cool before refrigerating. It can be used as soon as it is cold.

About keeping: Will keep for up to one week in the refrigerator.

Makes: About 750 ml/1¼ pints chocolate custard filling

USE FOR:
Chocolate Ribbon
Cake
Custard-filled
Chocolate
Chip Eclairs
Layered Custard
Cream Parfaits
Meringue and
Chocolate
Chequerboard
Poached Pears with
Gold Leaves

EQUIPMENT:
Kitchen scales
Measuring jug
Sieve
2 medium bowls
Whisk
Heavy-based
saucepan
Rubber spatula
Slotted wooden
spatula
Cling film

21 *Chocolate-Hazelnut Tart Filling*

USE FOR:
Chocolate-Hazelnut
Tart
Chocolate-Hazelnut
Shortbread Squares
(Assorted Biscuits
and Sweets)

EQUIPMENT:
Kitchen scales
Large chef's knife
Food processor
Measuring jug
Rubber spatula
Medium bowl
Whisk

INGREDIENTS:

250 g/8 oz hazelnuts, toasted and
rubbed to remove skins (see
Technique Notes, page 10)
140 g/5 oz dark brown sugar
125 g/4 oz unsalted butter
3 eggs
60 g/2 oz unsweetened or
bittersweet chocolate, melted and
cooled
165 g/5½ oz golden syrup
2 teaspoons vanilla essence
2 tablespoons Frangelico liqueur

INSTRUCTIONS:

1 Lightly chop the hazelnuts. You
can process them in a food processor,
but I prefer to chop by hand with a
large, heavy knife to control the size
of the pieces. Larger bits are nicer in
the tart; if making hazelnut squares,
smaller pieces will make the squares
easier to cut.

2 Cream the brown sugar and butter
together in a food processor. Add the
eggs and chocolate and process until
smooth.

3 Scrape the mixture into a medium
bowl. Whisk in syrup, vanilla essence
and liqueur. Stir in the nuts. From
here follow assembly for Chocolate-
Hazelnut Tart, page 48, or
Chocolate-Hazelnut Shortbread
Squares, page 57 .

About keeping: Use immediately.

Makes: About 750 g/25 oz filling

22 *Tangerine Curd*

USE FOR:
Custard-filled Chocolate
Chip Eclairs
Layered Chocolate
Angel Food Cake
Meringue and Chocolate
Chequerboard
Mexican Chocolate
Custard Cake

EQUIPMENT:
Kitchen scales
Medium bowl over
medium saucepan
Measuring jug
Small bowl
Whisk
Rubber spatula
Cling film

NOTES:

Ring the changes on traditional
lemon curd with other frozen fruit
juice concentrates.

INGREDIENTS:

125 g/4 oz unsalted butter
100 g/3½ oz sugar
125 g/4 oz tangerine or orange juice
concentrate
Finely grated rind of 2 tangerines
(optional)
2 whole eggs
4 egg yolks

INSTRUCTIONS:

1 Melt the butter with the sugar, juice
contrate and rind in a bowl over a
saucepan a quarter full of simmering
water. Whisk until smooth.

2 Whisk the eggs and egg yolks

together in a small bowl, then stir
into the hot mixture. Continue to stir
with a rubber spatula, scraping the
sides and bottom of the bowl. The
curd will go through a lumpy stage
but smooth out again as it thickens.
When the thickening stops in 5-10
minutes, transfer the curd to a
storage container and cover with
cling film to prevent a skin from
forming. Cool before refrigerating.

About keeping: Will keep for up to
one week in the refrigerator.

Makes: About 500 g/16 oz curd

White Chocolate Ganache

23

NOTES:

Crème fraîche helps cut the sweetness of the white chocolate, although you may use double cream instead, if you like.

INGREDIENTS:

250 g/8 oz white chocolate
150 ml/5 fl oz crème fraîche

INSTRUCTIONS:

1 Melt the chocolate in small bowl over a medium saucepan a quarter full of simmering water. Whisk until smooth.

2 Remove the bowl from the saucepan and whisk in the *crème fraîche*. Set aside to cool until its texture is suitable to use; if piping, you may want to refrigerate it briefly.

About keeping: Can be stored refrigerated for up to six weeks, re-melt and then cool to bring to a proper working texture.

Makes: About 400 g/14 oz ganache

USE FOR:
Chocolate Ribbon Cake
Layered Chocolate Angel Food Cake
Lightning Bolt
Dacquoise
Whiskey-Apricot Chocolate Torte

EQUIPMENT:
Kitchen scales
Small bowl over medium saucepan
Measuring jug
Whisk

Dark Chocolate Ganache

24

NOTES:

An alternate to this recipe's food processor method for melting the chocolate with the cream is the use of a bowl over hot water. However, to melt that last lump of chocolate over water takes so much more heat that the ganache takes much longer to cool enough to use.

INGREDIENTS:

250 g/8 oz dark chocolate
125 ml/4 fl oz double cream
2 tablespoons golden syrup

INSTRUCTIONS:

1 Chop the chocolate into small chunks and place in a food processor.

2 Bring the cream to the boil and pour immediately over the chocolate in the food processor. You may want to hold a towel round the lid of the machine to start - it is initially rough and splattery. Process until all the lumps of chocolate have been melted. Add the syrup and blend to combine.

The ganache will be a perfect consistency for glazing cakes; a few minutes refrigeration will bring it to piping texture.

About keeping: Can be stored in the refrigerator for up to six weeks; re-melt and then cool to bring to a proper working texture.

Makes: About 350 g/12 oz ganache

USE FOR:
Layered Chocolate Angel Food Cake
Lightning Bolt
Dacquoise
Meringue and Chocolate Chequerboard
Whiskey-Apricot Chocolate Torte

EQUIPMENT
Kitchen scales
Heavy knife
Food processor
Small saucepan

25 *Whipped Cream*

USE FOR:
Chocolate-Chocolate
 Mousse Torte
Chocolate Pancakes
 with Flambéed
 Oranges
Chocolate-Hazelnut
 Tart
Chocolate Pastry
 Latticed Apricot Tart
Chocolate Ribbon
 Cake
Custard-filled
 Chocolate Chip
 Eclairs
Layered Custard
 Cream Parfaits
Mexican Chocolate
 Custard Cake

EQUIPMENT:
Electric mixer and
 bowl, chilled

NOTES:

It may seem presumptuous to offer a recipe for one of the first things a child is allowed to do in the kitchen. Yet few things are so often done badly - over- sweetened, over- whipped or abandoned completely for commercial versions. These proportions and hints will make every batch pipe like silk, dollop like a cloud and last for hours, if necessary. In what must have been its ultimate test, a whipped cream covered five-tier wedding cake for more than 500 people remained intact in a garden gazebo for 3½ hours one hot and sunny August day. I can think of no higher recommendation; it's served me well.

INGREDIENTS:

250 ml/5 fl oz double cream, well
 chilled
1 tablespoon icing sugar
1 teaspoon vanilla essence

INSTRUCTIONS:

1 The most crucial thing to remember is to whip slowly. The electric mixers that bade farewell to the ache in the whisking arms gave us more power than we need when it comes to cream, and we use too much. Beat at medium speed - the air bubbles trapped between the fat molecules will be finer, stronger and more durable and will achieve greater volume.

2 As soon as the first faint ridges left in the wake of the beaters appear on the surface of the cream, add first the icing sugar, then the vanilla. Whip to the texture appropriate for use intended.

About keeping: Don't let my anecdote about the wedding cake act as license to abuse - whipped cream should be kept cold for as long as possible before serving. While it will hold piped for several hours, it should be whipped just before piping to ensure a smooth flow. If it must stand for even a few minutes before entering the piping bag, whisk first to smooth.

Makes: About 500 ml/16 fl oz whipped cream

Whipped Crème Fraîche

NOTES:

Prepared *crème fraîche* is now available in many supermarkets; if not in yours, it's easy enough to make at home. Buttermilk is the sour-tasting liquid left after milk has been churned to butter. In this recipe, it provides the culture to thicken the cream. Look for buttermilk in health food shops. Because *crème fraîche* is thicker to begin with it whips to only about half the volume of the same amount of uncultured cream.

INGREDIENTS:

60 ml/2 fl oz buttermilk
250 ml/S fl oz double cream
2 tablespoons icing sugar

INSTRUCTIONS:

1 Mix the buttermilk with the double cream in a jar and cover loosely to keep out any dust. Set in a warm – but not hot – place for 24 hours, until the mixture is thick but still drops from a spoon in fine strings.

2 Cover and chill the mixture; it will thicken more when cold.

3 To whip, add the icing sugar and whip at medium speed. It will look thinner at first, then develop a stiff-peak texture, heavier than that of whipped cream.

About keeping: Crème fraîche unwhipped and refrigerated will keep for up to a week; whipped, for several hours. Although it should always be whipped as close to serving time as possible, it does maintain a better texture for longer than whipped cream.

Makes: About 350 ml/12 fl oz whipped *crème fraîche*

USE FOR:
Chocolate Pancakes
with Flambéed
Oranges
Chocolate Ribbon
Cake
Fruit and Cream
with Chocolate
Triangles
Layered Chocolate
Angel Food Cake
Mexican Chocolate
Custard Cake
Poached Pears with
Gold Leaves

EQUIPMENT:
Measuring jug
500 ml/16 fl oz
glass jar
Measuring spoons
Electric mixer
and bowl

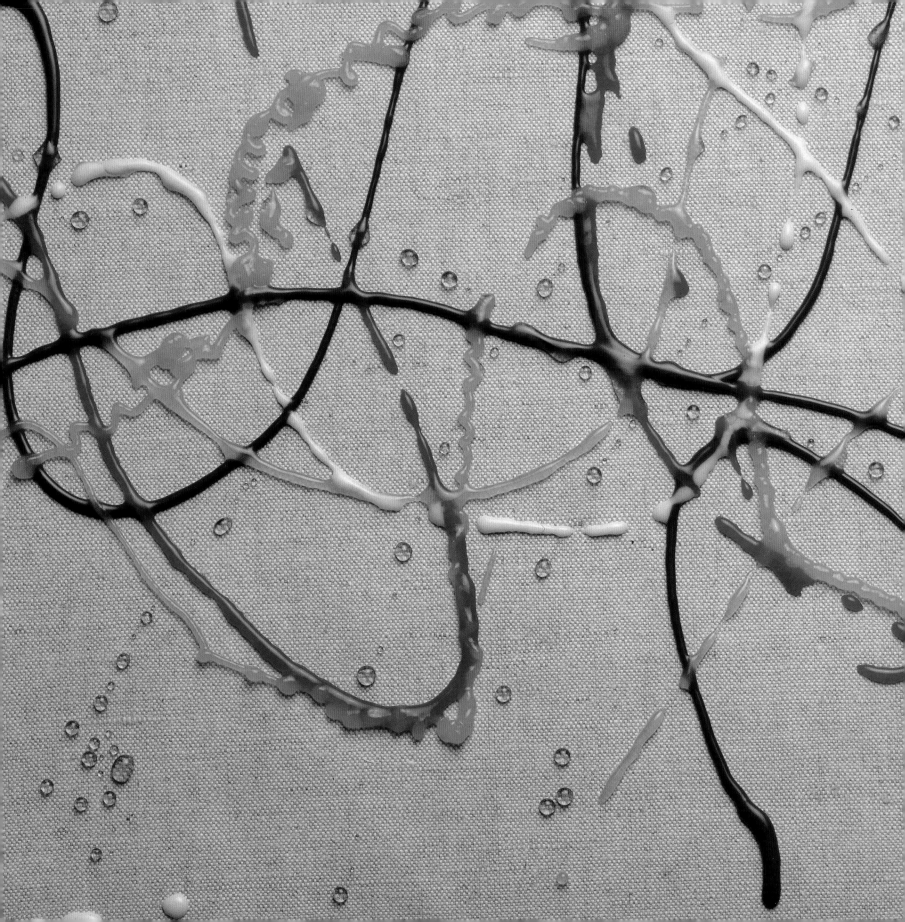

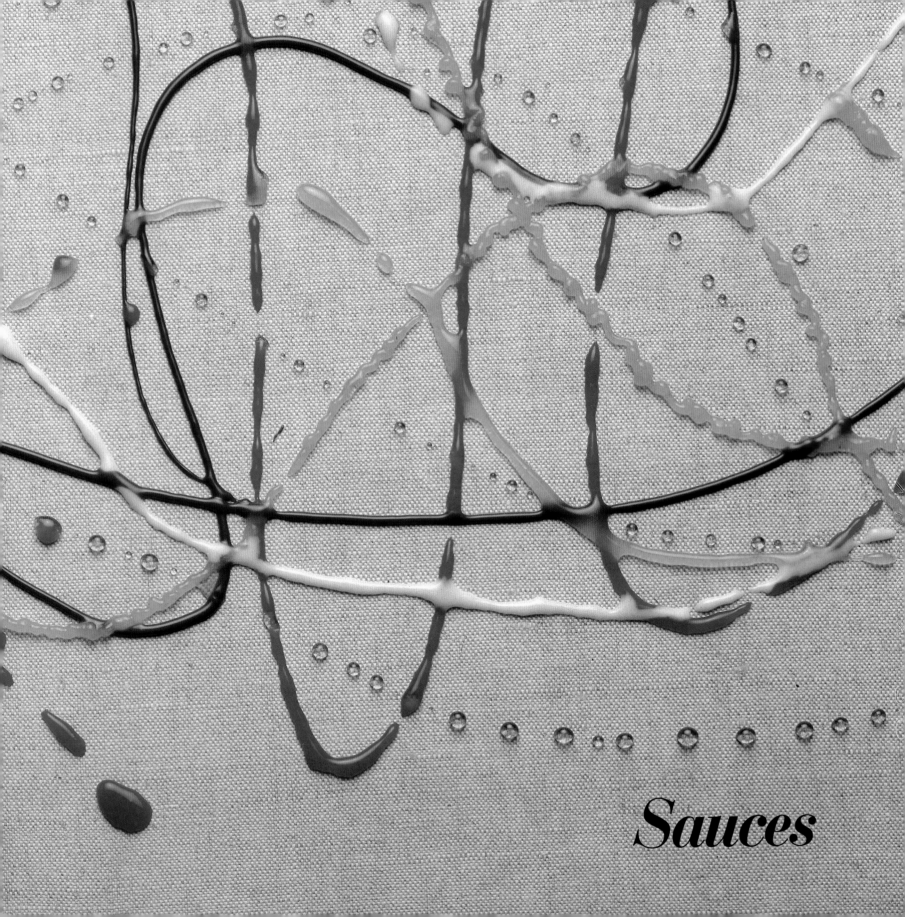

Sauces

27 *Chocolate-Cognac Sauce*

USE FOR:
Custard-filled
 Chocolate Chip
 Eclairs
Joan Collins'
 Broken Heart
Poached Pears with
 Gold Leaves

EQUIPMENT:
Kitchen scales
Medium bowl over
 medium saucepan
Whisk
Measuring jug
Measuring spoons

INGREDIENTS:

250 g/8 oz dark chocolate
125 ml/4 fl oz milk
2 tablespoons golden syrup
2 tablespoons Cognac

INSTRUCTIONS:

1 Melt the chocolate in medium bowl over a medium saucepan a quarter full of simmering water.

2 Whisk in the milk until smooth, then add the syrup and Cognac.

3 Warm to slightly above room temperature to serve; the sauce should pour but not spread on plate.

About keeping: Will keep for up to six weeks in the refrigerator.

Makes: About 400 ml/14 fl oz sauce

28 *Bitter Orange Sauce*

USE FOR:
Joan Collins'
 Broken Heart
Mexican Chocolate
 Custard Cake
Mocha Mousse
 with Bitter Orange
 Sauce
Poached Pears
 with Gold Leaves
Raspberries with
 Custard and Fruit
 Sauces

EQUIPMENT:
Kitchen scales
Small saucepan
Measuring spoons
Wooden spoon

NOTES:

'Bitter' here refers not to the fruit called the bitter orange but to this sauce's sharp flavour. Its lack of sweetness allows it not only to cut the sweetness of other components in a dessert but to make a terrific addition to meat glazes and marinades.

INGREDIENTS:

180 g/6 oz frozen orange juice
 concentrate, thawed
70 g/2⅓ oz sugar
1 tablespoon Grand Marnier

INSTRUCTIONS:

1 Combine the thawed concentrate, sugar and Grand Marnier in a small saucepan.

2 Stir the ingredients and bring to the boil over medium-high heat. Boil, stirring constantly, for 2 minutes or until the sauce is reduced to about 180 ml/6 fl oz.

3 Chill before using.

About keeping: Will keep for several months in the refrigerator.

Makes: About 180 ml/6 fl oz sauce

Raspberry Sauce

NOTES:

This is the most luxurious of all fruit sauces, for here we cheat nature by removing the thorns on the rose of the fruit world – the seeds of the raspberry. Most raspberry sauces depend so much on sugar and thickening agents to achieve proper texture that they dull the fruit's naturally sharp flavour. Here the sauce is thickened with the pulp of the berries themselves, creating a fruity, velvety, gleaming sauce worth making for the aroma in your kitchen alone! Remember all fresh raspberries are not created equal; you may need to reduce the sauce more or less depending on their moisture content.

INGREDIENTS:

500 g/1 lb fresh raspberries
2 tablespoons water
50 g/1⅔ oz sugar
2 tablespoons golden syrup

INSTRUCTIONS:

1 Put the raspberries and water in a saucepan and bring to the boil over a medium heat. Use a wooden spoon to stir in the sugar, and cook for 5 minutes, until the berries are completely broken down.

2 Pour the berries into a sieve over a small bowl; set aside to cool. Press as much of the remaining juice and pulp through the sieve until nothing remains in the sieve but dry seeds. You may use a spoon or rubber spatula for this, but the best tool here is your fingers, rubbing the pulp up the sides of the sieve. Occasionally scrape the accumulation on the underside into the juice. You may need to repeat this to remove all the seeds; if you do, whisk the strained raspberries first.

3 Whisk the pulp and juice together with the syrup, then return to the saucepan. Cook over a medium heat for another 10 minutes to clear sauce and reduce it to about 250 ml/8 fl oz. Pour into a storage container and cool, then refrigerate. Serve cold.

About keeping: Will last for up to two weeks in the refrigerator but if re-boiled weekly it will last for several weeks longer.

Makes: About 250 ml/8 fl oz sauce

USE FOR:
Chocolate-Chocolate
Mousse Torte
Custard-filled
Chocolate Chip
Eclairs
Joan Collins'
Broken Heart
Layered Custard
Cream Parfaits
Mango and
Chocolate Sorbets
Mexican Chocolate
Custard Cake
Mocha Mousse with
Bitter Orange Sauce
Poached Pears with
Gold Leaves
Raspberries with
Custard and
Fruit Sauces

EQUIPMENT:
Kitchen scales
Small saucepan
Measuring spoons
Wooden spoon
Fine mesh nylon sieve
Small bowl
Whisk

30 *Apricot Sauce*

USE FOR:
Joan Collins'
  Broken Heart
Mexican Chocolate
  Custard Cake
Raspberries with
  Custard and Fruit
  Sauces

EQUIPMENT:
Can opener
Measuring jug
Food processor or
  blender
Rubber spatula
Medium saucepan
Wooden spoon
Sieve
Measuring spoons

NOTES:

This piquant, velvety fruit sauce is so versatile it even finds its way into my Oriental stir-fry sauces, it not only lends flavour but acts as a thickening agent as well.

INGREDIENTS:

1 x 425 g/14 oz can stoned apricot halves in syrup
1 tablespoon brandy

INSTRUCTIONS:

1 Drain the syrup from the apricots into a measuring jug.

2 Combine the apricots with 120 ml/ 4 fl oz of the syrup in a food processor or blender. Purée until smooth.

3 Scrape the purée into a medium saucepan and bring to the boil over a medium heat. Cook for 5 minutes, stirring occasionally with a wooden spoon until reduced to about 350 ml/ 12 fl oz.

4 Strain into a storage container, then stir in brandy. Cool, then refrigerate. Serve cold.

About keeping: Will keep for several months in the refrigerator.

Makes: About 250 ml/8 fl oz sauce

Vanilla Custard Sauce

NOTES:

This is one of the more difficult basic sauces to master only because it's one of those where you know you had it right only after you've already cooked it for too long. It should be as thick as it can be without curdling the egg and making it grainy – it should never boil. If you have gone so far that even whisking over ice water doesn't help to return its lustre, a quick whizz in a food processor may still work to make it smooth.

While the custard is cooling, cover the surface with a piece of cling film to prevent a skin from forming.

INGREDIENTS:

300 ml/10 fl oz milk
2 teaspoons vanilla essence
5 egg yolks
100 g/3¼ oz sugar

INSTRUCTIONS:

1 Scald the milk in heavy-based medium saucepan just until a skin forms. Remove from the heat and add the vanilla essence.

2 Beat the egg yolks and sugar with an electric mixer at high speed until they are nearly white. Add one third of the hot milk and beat again slowly to combine.

3 Return the milk and egg yolks to the milk in the saucepan. Cook over a medium-low heat, stirring constantly with a slotted wooden spatula, until the sauce thickens slightly and holds a line drawn with your fingertip in a coating of sauce on the back of a metal spoon.

4 When the sauce is done, transfer it to a metal bowl partially immersed in ice water, then continue stirring to reduce the temperature rapidly and stop the cooking. Pour into a storage container and cool, then refrigerate.

About keeping: Will keep for up to one week in the refrigerator.

Makes: About 500 ml/16 fl oz sauce

USE FOR:
Mexican Choclate
Custard Cake
Poached Pears with
Gold leaves
Rasperries with
Custard and Fruit
Sauces

EQUIPMENT:
Kitchen Scales
Measuring jug
Heavy-based medium
saucepan
Measuring spoons
Electric mixer and
bowl
Slotted wooden
spatula
Metal spoon
Medium metal
bowl partially
immersed in ice
water

Little Sweets & Extras

32 *Whiskey Prunes in Chocolate*

USE FOR:
Assorted Biscuits and
  Sweets

EQUIPMENT:
Measuring jug
Deep small bowl
Medium sauté pan
Slotted spoon
Wire rack over
  baking sheet
Small bowl over
  saucepan
Whisk
Baking parchment
125 ml/4 fl oz cup or
  ramekin
Wooden skewer

INGREDIENTS:

25 ml/4 fl oz bourbon whiskey
20 large stoned prunes, about 180 g/
  6 oz
50 g/1⅔ oz sugar
125 g/4 oz milk chocolate

INSTRUCTIONS:

1 Pour the whiskey into a deep bowl, add the prunes and soak for 24 hours.

2 Pour the whiskey and prunes into a sauté pan, add the sugar and bring to the boil over a medium heat. Ignite and burn off the alcohol, shaking the pan constantly.

3 Turn the heat to low, then continue to reduce the liquid, for 10 minutes, shaking the pan occasionally.

4 As the glaze gets thick and sticky and begins to caramelize, remove the prunes with a slotted spoon. Drain on a wire rack over a baking sheet, then cool.

5 Melt the chocolate in a small bowl over a saucepan a quarter full of simmering water. Whisk until smooth.

6 Remove the wire rack, scrape the drips of sugar off the baking sheet and line it with baking parchment. Scrape the chocolate into a small cup to make dipping easier. Spear each prune with a wooden skewer, then dip it two-thirds of the way into the chocolate. Lift it, shake and place on the baking parchment. Allow to set in a cool place. Do not refrigerate (moisture condensation loosens and spots chocolate).

About keeping: This sweet will be at its most attractive served soon after dipping. They can be kept in an airtight container for several weeks. Although the chocolate may discolour, the flavour will not be affected.

Makes: 20 dipped prunes

Pistachio Brittle on Chocolate

INGREDIENTS:

125 g/4 oz shelled pistachios
60 ml/2 fl oz water
150 g/5 oz sugar
About 1½ tablespoons butter
¼ teaspoon bicarbonate of soda
180 g/6 oz bittersweet chocolate

INSTRUCTIONS:

1 Spread the nuts on a baking sheet and place in a 180°C/350°F/Gas 4 oven for 5–10 minutes to toast lightly. Place on a tea towel and rub to blot the excess oil. Wipe off the baking sheet and rub with ½ tablespoon butter.

2 Add the water, then the sugar to a saucepan on the hob – do not move or stir these, to prevent any sugar crystals from sticking to sides. Bring to the boil over a medium heat, then continue to cook without stirring until the sugar caramelizes. Watch it carefully.

3 As the sugar reaches a golden brown colour remove it from the heat and stir in at once the nuts, remaining butter and the bicarbonate of soda using a wooden spoon – the mixture will foam up. Begin spooning about 20 small clusters of nut brittle on to the buttered baking sheet. Cool for at least 15 minutes, until the brittle is hard and cool enough to handle.

4 Melt the chocolate in a small bowl over a small saucepan a quarter full of simmering water. Stir until smooth. Line a second baking sheet with baking parchment and spoon 2.5 cm/1 in dollops of chocolate on to it – as many as you have nut clusters. Gently loosen the nut clusters by twisting them. Wipe the base of each with some kitchen towel to remove the butter, then push it into a pool of melted chocolate until the chocolate shows around the edge. Allow to set in a cool place before peeling off the baking parchment.

About keeping: Can be kept in an airtight container in a cool, dark place.

Makes: About 20 sweets

USE FOR:
Assorted Biscuits
and Sweets

EQUIPMENT:
Kitchen scales
2 baking sheets
Tea towel
Measuring jug
and spoons
Medium saucepan
Wooden spoon
Baking parchment
Small bowl over
small saucepan
Spoon
Kitchen towels

34 *Poached Pears*

USE FOR:

Chocolate
  Tortellini in Pear
  Syrup
Poached Pears with
  Gold Leaves

EQUIPMENT:

Kitchen scales
Paring knife
Medium bowl
Vegetable peeler
Melon baller
Large saucepan
  with lid
Slotted spoon
  (if necessary)
Baking sheet
  (if necessary)

NOTES:

The sweet, juicy Conference and the rich and aromatic Comise pears are the most popular varieties in Britain, and both are suitable for poaching. If you come across juicy Bartletts or the sturdy Boses and d'Anjous in your market, they also work well. Any of these can be used here, though the softer types or very ripe pears of any variety require greater care in handling to prevent scarring (bruises do not go away) and a far shorter cooking time. As a general rule, pears that are not quite ripe enough to eat raw are best. But all pears beg to be poached, for two important reasons. Since they brown and bruise easily, pears need the double protection of being kept from the air and being slightly glazed by the sugar. And, although the flesh retains its shape well when cooked, the sponge-like texture has a tendency to dissipate pears' moisture content; it is best to cook and store them suspended in liquid until serving to keep them plump, firm and juicy.

Although pears are most often poached in red wine, I find the colour unpleasant after they are drained for serving and dry off a bit. Also, often the colour doesn't completely penetrate, which causes problems if you need to trim, slice or fan the fruit for presentation. A perfect match is found in wedding the flavours of pear and the white wine Chardonnay, and the mellow golden colour the pears assume is very appealing.

For enough poaching liquid to make Chocolate Tortellini in Pear Syrup (18) double the amounts of wine and cinnamon and add pear or apple juice. If you can't find clear pear juice, apple juice will provide a transparent syrup, although a less intense pear flavour. (You'll still have 4 extra pear halves; use them to top green salads with toasted nuts and a tart dressing.)

INGREDIENTS:

2 lemons
5 well shaped pears
1 bottle white wine, preferably
  Chardonnay
1 stick cinnamon
150 g/5 oz sugar

For Chocolate Tortellini in Pear Syrup:
750 ml/1¼ pints pear juice or apple
  juice

INSTRUCTIONS:

1 Halve and squeeze the lemons into a medium bowl, half-filled with water then add the rind.

2 To prepare the pears, cut off the stalks and pare out the blossom ends. Peel the pears; a paring knife is fine, but a vegetable peeler gives smoother results. Halve the pears, then scoop out, seed pocket with melon baller, and remove the stem fibres with a 'V' shaped notch cut from the hole to the stalk end. Immediately put each half in the lemon water.

3 Bring the wine, cinnamon and sugar (and pear juice, if making Chocolate Tortellini in Pear Syrup) to the boil in a large saucepan. Add the pears and, if necessary, some of the lemon water to cover. Return to a simmer, cover and cook for 5–20 minutes until the pears can be pierced with a fork at the seed cavity but are still firm. The time depends on the pears' ripeness and variety.

4 If the pears are just right at this point, remove the saucepan from the heat and set aside to cool, uncovered, before transferring to a storage container for refrigerating. Or, if the pears have already started to soften and are easily pierced with a fork, carefully lift out each pear half with a slotted spoon and lay it on a baking sheet to cool quickly; cool the poaching liquid separately, then add it to the pears for storage.

About keeping: Will keep for several weeks in the refrigerator.

Makes: 10 poached pear halves

Moulded Mocha and Cream Mousse 35

INGREDIENTS:

60 ml/2 fl oz water
1 tablespoon powdered gelatine
300 ml/½ pint milk
70 g/2¼ oz sugar
4 egg yolks
1 teaspoon vanilla essence
2 tablespoons good-quality instant coffee granules
2 teaspoons chocolate essence
250 ml/8 fl oz double cream

INSTRUCTIONS:

1 Place the water in a small bowl and stir in the gelatine. Set aside to soften.

2 Heat the milk in a medium saucepan. Meanwhile, in a second small bowl, whisk the sugar vigorously into the egg yolks. As the milk forms a skin, whisk one third of it into the egg yolk mixture, then scrape that back into the saucepan of milk and continue whisking to combine.

3 Cook over a medium heat and stir with a wooden spoon until the mixture thickens slightly and holds a line drawn with your fingertip in a coating of it on the back of the spoon. Remove from the heat, add the softened gelatine and stir until the gelatine is completely dissolved.

4 You now have about 500 ml/ 16 fl oz of custard base. Measure 125 ml/4 fl oz of this into the first small bowl, and add ½ teaspoon of the vanilla essence. Pour the rest into a second small bowl and stir in the coffee, chocolate essence and the remaining ½ teaspoon vanilla essence.

5 Whip the cream with an electric mixer until stiff. As the plain vanilla custard begins to cool and thicken, fold in half the whipped cream. Pour this into the base of slightly wet 1 litre/1¾ pint mould. Refrigerate.

6 As the mocha custard begins to cool and thicken, fold in the remaining whipped cream. As soon as the vanilla mousse has set enough to support the mocha flavoured mixtures, top up the mould with the mocha mixture, smooth the surface. Cover and refrigerate overnight before unmoulding.

About keeping: Will keep for several days in the mould in the refrigerator.

Makes: 6 servings

USE FOR:
Mocha Mousse
with Bitter Orange
Sauce

EQUIPMENT:
Kitchen scales
Measuring jug
and spoons
2 small bowls
Medium saucepan
Whisk
Rubber spatula
Wooden spoon
Electric mixer
and bowl
1 litre/1¾ pint
mould

36 *Coeur à la Crème Mixture*

USE FOR:
Joan Collins'
 Broken Heart

EQUIPMENT:
Kitchen scales
Food processor
Measuring spoons
Electric mixer
 and bowl
Large bowl
Large rubber spatula

INGREDIENTS:

250 g/8 oz full fat soft cheese
250 g/8 oz cottage cheese
40 g/1¼ oz icing sugar
1 tablespoon vanilla essence
3 tablespoons Amaretto liqueur
250 ml/8 fl oz double cream

INSTRUCTIONS:

1 Pinch the cream cheese in small lumps and put into a food processor with the cottage cheese. icing sugar. vanilla essence and Amaretto. Blend 6–8 times. then run the machine until the mixture is fairly smooth but still grainy.

2 Whip the cream to the stiff-peak stage with an electric mixer.

3 Scrape the cheese mixture into a large bowl and fold in the whipped cream.

To mould the mixture. proceed with the directions under Joan Collins' Broken Heart. page 54.

About keeping: To preserve the texture that results when mixture sets. this should be moulded at once.

Makes: Sufficient for a 1 litre/1¾ pint mould.

37 *Chocolate Chip-Mint Ice Cream*

USE FOR:
Chocolate Chip-
 Mint Ice Cream
 Sandwiches

EQUIPMENT:
Kitchen scales
Electric mixer and
 bowl
Medium saucepan
Rubber spatula
Wooden Spoon
Measuring spoons
Ice cream maker
Two 1 litre/1¾ pint
 plastic freezerproof
 containers, 8.5 cm/
 3½ in square

INGREDIENTS:

2 eggs
140 g/4¾ oz sugar
400 ml/14 fl oz milk
500 ml/16 fl oz double cream
1 tablespoon vanilla essence
½ teaspoon mint essence
6 drops liquid green food colouring
*125 g/4 oz dark chocolate, finely
 chopped*

INSTRUCTIONS:

1 Beat the eggs and sugar together until nearly white. with an electric mixer.

2 Heat the milk just until a skin forms. Beat a third of it into the egg-sugar mixture. then stir that back into the milk remaining in the saucepan.

3 Cook over a medium heat. stirring constantly with a wooden spoon until the custard thickens slightly and holds a line drawn with your fingertip in a coating of sauce on the back of the spoon. Chill thoroughly for several hours.

4 Stir in cream. vanilla and mint essences. food colouring and finely chopped chocolate. Pour into an ice cream maker and follow the manufacturer's instructions. Pack finished ice cream into the square plastic freezerproof containers.

About keeping: Will keep for three months in the freezer.

Makes: About 1 litre/1¾ pints ice cream (8 slices. 7.5 x 7.5 x 2 cm/3 x 3 x ¾ in for ice cream sandwiches)

Chocolate Sorbet

38

INGREDIENTS:

100 g/3½ oz sugar
250 ml/8 fl oz water
2 tablespoons chocolate essence
125 ml/4 fl oz evaporated milk
2 egg whites
125 ml/4 fl oz double cream

INSTRUCTIONS:

1 Bring the sugar. water and chocolate essence to the boil in a medium saucepan over a medium heat. Cover. reduce the heat and simmer for 5 minutes. Uncover and cook for 1 minute more. then add the evaporated milk. Transfer to a medium bowl and chill for several hours before continuing.

2 Beat the egg whites with an electric mixer until soft peaks form. Fold the cream into the egg whites. then fold the egg whites into the chocolate mixture in a medium bowl.

3 Pour into an ice cream maker and follow the manufacturer's instructions.

About keeping: Will keep for 3 months in the freezer.

Makes: About 750 ml/1¼ pint sorbet

USE FOR:
Mango and
Chocolate Sorbets
Poached Pears
with Gold Leaves

EQUIPMENT:
Kitchen scales
Medium saucepan
with lid
Measuring
jug and spoons
Medium bowl
Rubber spatula
Electric mixer and bowl
Ice cream maker

Mango Sorbet

39

INGREDIENTS:

100 g/3½ oz sugar
250 ml/8 fl oz water
1 ripe mango
3 tablespoons lemon juice
125 ml/4 fl oz double cream

INSTRUCTIONS:

1 Bring the sugar and water to the boil in a medium saucepan over a medium heat. Cover. reduce the heat and simmer for 5 minutes.

2 Cut the mango in half round the stone. and scrape the pulp from the stone and skin to weigh 165 g/ 5½ oz. If you have less than this was add water. Purée the pulp with the simmered sugar and water in a blender or food processor. then scrape through a sieve with a rubber spatula to remove the tough fibres. Stir in the lemon juice. then the cream. Chill thoroughly for several hours.

3 Pour into an ice cream maker and follow the manufacturer's instructions.

About keeping: Will keep for 3 months in the freezer.

Makes: About 750 ml/1¼ pint sorbet

USE FOR:
Chocolate Chip-Mint
Ice Cream Sandwiches
Mango and Chocolate
Sorbets

EQUIPMENT:
Kitchen scales
Medium saucepan
with lid
Measuring jug and
spoons
Paring knife
Blender or food
processor
Sieve
Rubber spatula
Ice cream maker

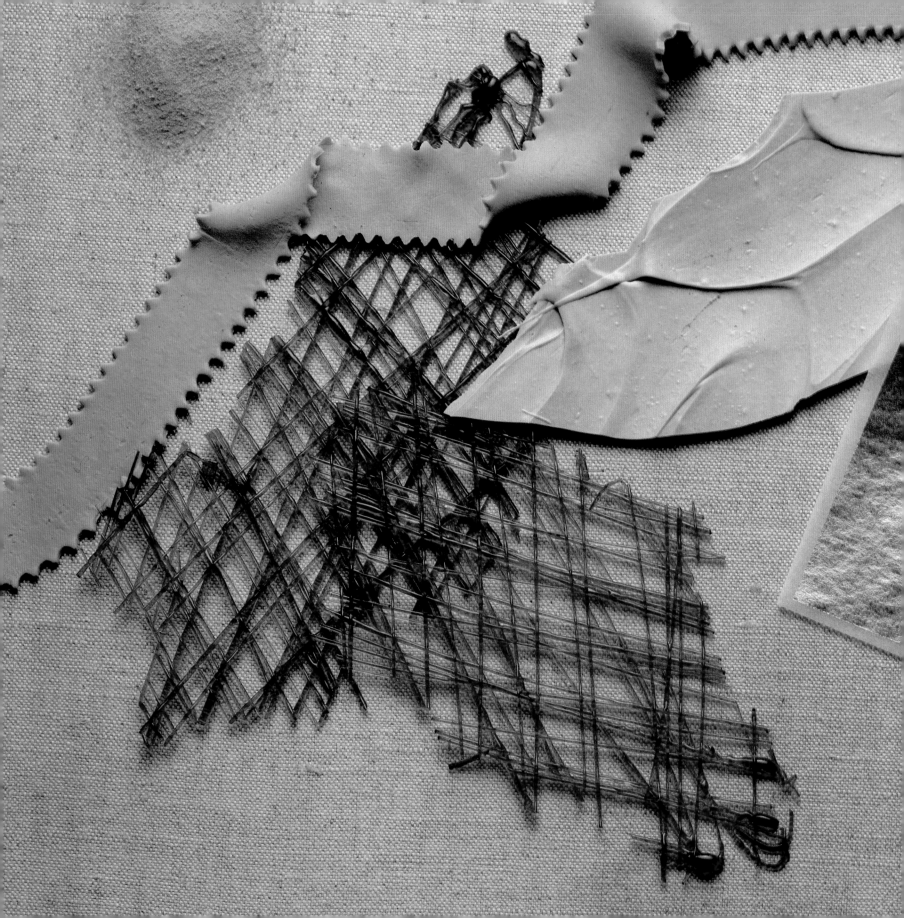

Accents & Decorations

40 *Chocolate Tiles*

Fruit and Cream
with Chocolate
Triangles
Joan Collins'
Broken Heart
Layered Chocolate
Angel Food Cake
Layered Custard
Cream Parfaits
Lightning Bolt
Dacquoise
Meringue and
Chocolate
Chequerboard
Poached Pears with
Gold Leaves
Raspberries with
Custard and Fruit
Sauces
Whiskey-Apricot
Chocolate Torte

NOTES:

Since I developed this versatile component several years ago it has become my trademark: I never seem to run out of new designs and applications, and there are so many left I doubt if I ever will. It has been everything from a sort of chip with dessert dips to 'icing' to decoration, and never fails to elicit an amazed, delighted response.

'Tiles' are any shape you cut or break from a base sheet of chocolate, which you create as described here. The sheet may be of dark, white or tinted chocolate, and be top-decorated or not. Sheet-top decorations may be the drizzle, stripes, marble effect, gilding or smears you're guided here to reproduce or any other design that you invent.

Because dark chocolate has a lower melting temperature than white it is more difficult to work with in this form, and its uses are restricted. Among these recipes it's called for only in Joan Collins' Broken Heart (page 54): the fact that this dessert is kept cold makes the use of dark chocolate more practical. The material that offers most flexibility, especially when you use a scalpel to cut precise shapes, is cake covering. It contains no cocoa butter at all but is similar in look and taste to chocolate and is far superior in handling – smooth and firm, not brittle.

What follows are instructions for creating the basic chocolate sheet, then additional instructions for achieving each of the variations pictured in this book, followed by instructions for cooling and then cutting and breaking the sheet into tiles. Though the technique is straightforward, working with chocolate always requires attention to detail; please read through the instructions once before you start.

INGREDIENTS:

Small amount vegetable oil
250–275 g/8–9 oz white or dark chocolate for one base sheet plain chocolate
Food colouring (preferably commercial paste or powder; see Ingredients Notes)

For adding sheet-top decorative chocolate:
60 g/2 oz extra chocolate for each colour (the minimum for convenient melting; actually apply no more than 125 g/4 oz total)

INSTRUCTIONS:

To make a base sheet:
1 Smear the back of a baking sheet with the oil, then top with a pan-sized sheet of baking parchment so it clings to the pan but has no oil on top. Be sure the parchment has no ridges or air bubbles.

2 Melt the chocolate in a bowl over a saucepan a quarter filled with simmering water. You'll need one bowl each for white and dark chocolate if using both, but you can melt their contents one at a time as called for in the variations. Whisk until smooth .

For tinted white chocolate, add colour. First ladle any white chocolate that you're tinting for sheet-top decoration only into one or more small cups. Then, if using paste, with toothpicks or skewers transfer a very small amount (it's strong!) of the colour into each cup of chocolate, and stir with a spoon to blend the colour evenly.

3 Scrape the smoothed warm chocolate on to the parchment paper. It is a good idea – especially for first attempts – to warm the pan over a gas flame slightly to extend your working time. Spread the chocolate to all the corners and then from end to end from both long sides with a palette knife to create a smooth layer of chocolate slightly less than 3 mm/⅛ in. thick.

4 With white or tinted white chocolate only, once you've spread a smooth layer proceed with a variation, A through E, if desired. Note that all the variations require a still-soft base sheet except those which use gold; in these variations the base sheet should be cooled thoroughly before the application.

To vary the base sheet:
A To apply dark chocolate drizzle (as for Fruit and Cream with Chocolate Triangles, page 42): Put a small amount of melted dark chocolate in a strong freezer bag, and cut a small hole in the corner. While the chocolate base sheet is still soft, pipe on a random pattern of drizzle. Do not tap the pan to smooth as in variations using white sheet-top chocolate; since dark chocolate is softer, tapping would cause the sheet

to break along the lines of the drizzle.

B To apply marbling (as in Layered Chocolate Angel Food Cake, page 46): Use small amounts of extra melted chocolate that you've tinted in one or more contrasting colours. Dip your fingertip in each colour and fling it at the still soft base sheet to form spatter patterns. Then draw a skewer through the entire surface in random patterns to swirl and 'pull' the colours. If the chocolate has already begun to set, warm the pan over a gas flame to re-soften. Rap the pan sharply to smooth out the surface.

C To apply stripes for drawn stripes or zigzags: Scrape each sheet top chocolate tint you're using into a small, strong freezer bag, and cut a small hole in the corner of each. Pipe alternating stripes across the length of the pan into the still soft base sheet.

For drawn stripes (as in front half of Lightning Bolt Dacquoise, page 16) draw a skewer through the stripes in a series of loops a few stripes wide from end to end. Repeat all the way down and across the pan.

For a zigzag effect (as in Raspberries with Custard and Fruit Sauces, page 30) draw a skewer in a repeating 'W' pattern across a few stripes at a time along the length of the pan, then come back across the pan a short distance beneath the first line in the opposite direction. Reverse and go back again to the bottom of the sheet.

Rap the pan sharply on the edge of your work surface to smooth any surface irregularities in the chocolate.

D To apply contrasting smears (as on one decoration for Layered Custard Cream Parfaits, page 52): Use extra melted white chocolate that you've tinted in one or more contrasting colours; drip these in small amounts at random points across the base sheet. Smear the chocolate back and forth from end to end, from each long side of the pan with a palette knife. You'll have only two or three passes before the colours begin to muddy, so make the most of them.

E To gild or accent with gold: Gold for gilding may be found at graphics or art supply shops catering to designers and sign makers. Though difficult to deal with, gold instills a sense of wonder and luxury like nothing else will. It has been used as a garnish in India for centuries; look for gold and silver food decorations at Indian shops; both colours are called *vark*. The easiest form to use comes attached to squares of parchment paper, said to be for 'gilding in the wind' – ask for it by name.

To gild (as for Poached Pears with Gold Leaves, page 50) lay the gold-covered parchment paper gold side down on a well-set chocolate base sheet. Rub your finger carefully back and forth across the back of the sheet; the gold will adhere to the surface of the chocolate. Lift off the paper.

To accent tiles with gold (as in one of the decorations on Layered Custard Cream Parfait, page 52), first cut individual tiles so you know where you want the gold to go. Lay the gold-covered parchment paper over the tiles, gold side down, and draw a zigzag pattern on to each tile to press a line of the gold on to the surface of the chocolate. Lift off the paper and brush off any excess gold.

To cool the completed sheet and cut or break into tiles:
Put the chocolate sheet in a cool place to set. Once dark chocolate is set at room temperature you may still need to refrigerate it momentarily to make it firm enough to cut. Never, however, refrigerate either form of white chocolate. Either form will pick up moisture or, as it returns to room temperature, water will condense on it; this may spot the chocolate and will make colours run.

To cut into tiles, use a ruler and a scalpel found in art supply shops.

To break into tiles, lift the entire sheet of chocolate, peel back the parchment paper and break off pieces.

About keeping: Will keep for several weeks covered in a cool, dark place.

Makes: One base sheet

EQUIPMENT:
30 x 42.5 x 2.5 cm/ 12 x 17 x 1 in Swiss roll tin or baking sheet
Baking parchment
Medium bowl (or bowls) over medium saucepan
Whisk
Rubber spatula
Palette knife

For adding tints:
Wooden cocktail sticks or small skewers
Spoon for each colour

For handling sheet-top decorative white chocolate:
Ladle
Small cups for mixing colours

Also:
Small, strong freezer bags for piping (variations A and C)
Gold (variation E; see notes)

41 *Spiced Ground Orange Peel*

USE FOR:
Chocolate Pancakes
  with Flambéed
  Oranges
Chocolate Tortellini
  in Pear Broth
Poached Pears with
  Gold Leaves

EQUIPMENT:
Vegetable peeler
Parchment lined
  baking sheet
Electric coffee or
  spice grinder

NOTES:

This gorgeous, saffron-coloured powder is useful in desserts, as a garnish or even in most savoury cooking where a hint of orange is desired. If you find particularly well coloured oranges make more – it will keep until you use it up.

INGREDIENTS:

3–4 large, well-coloured oranges
½ teaspoon ground cardamom

INSTRUCTIONS:

1 Cut the orange part of skin from the oranges with a vegetable peeler (which allows the precise control of thickness you need). Lay strips of peel on baking parchment lined baking sheet with outer skin side up. Place in 120°C/250°F/Gas ½ oven for 30 minutes or until they are crisp when cool, but not browned. Open the oven door a few times to release any moisture, and to release the aroma into the kitchen!

2 When cool, combine the orange peel with the cardamom in the spice grinder and grind to a fine powder.

About keeping: Lasts up to three months if kept in the freezer.

Makes: 2 tablespoons ground peel

42 *Chocolate Filigree*

USE FOR:
Layered Custard
  Cream Parfaits
Poached Pears
  with Gold Leaves

EQUIPMENT:
Small bowl over
  saucepan
30 x 42.5 x 2.5 cm/
  12 x 17 x 1 in Swiss
  roll tin or baking
  sheet
Baking parchment
Rubber spatula
Small, strong
  freezer bag

NOTES:

This is perhaps the easiest garnish in this book for the amount of drama it produces. There is no need to spend hours perfecting exact replicas of classic fans and rosettes. Naively drawn atoms, stars, lattice or just an overall Jackson Pollock squiggle and spatter that's randomly broken can be far more interesting.

INGREDIENTS:

90 g/3 oz chocolate
Few drops vegetable oil

INSTRUCTIONS:

1 Melt the chocolate in a bowl over a saucepan a quarter full of simmering water. Smear the back of a baking sheet with vegetable oil, then smooth a pan-size sheet of baking parchment on to it.

2 Spoon the chocolate into a plastic bag. Cut a very small hole at the corner; test the thickness of line it produces and increase the size of the hole if necessary to achieve the effect you desire. Pipe out filigree designs – enjoy yourself!

3 Set the chocolate in a cool place to firm, but do not refrigerate. Lift up the parchment paper and gently peel back to free the shapes or break the pieces of the filigree sheet.

About keeping: Make the same day as serving; in time, chocolate may discolour.

Makes: 1 sheet filigree

Chocolate Decorations

NOTES:

Unlike flat chocolate tiles, this form of chocolate decoration allows for three dimensional effects. It is also easier in this form than others to use dark chocolate, if you'd like, though the possibilities for tinting are more limited. The decorations will attach readily to most dessert surfaces; whipped cream would be too wet, but ganache, buttercream or chocolate all make a fine base.

INGREDIENTS:

125 g/4 oz chocolate, white or dark
For tinted white chocolate, paste
* food colourings (see Ingredients*
* Notes)*
2 tablespoons golden syrup

INSTRUCTIONS:

1 Melt the chocolate in a small bowl over a medium saucepan a quarter full of simmering water.

If you're using white chocolate and want to tint it, stir in a tiny amount of colouring now. You'll have to settle for pastels, since extra dye will seize up the chocolate before you can incorporate the syrup, and for this mixture you can't use the trick of adding oil to re-smooth it.

2 Stir in the syrup, just barely combining. It will seize up violently. Wrap and refrigerate for one hour.

3 Remove the chocolate from the refrigerator and begin working it with your (impeccably clean) hands. Roll out half of the batch at a time to make a 7.5 x 23 cm/3 x 9 in strip. If it's sticky, re-chill; if it is still sticky, your slab may be too warm. If that is not the case, or if you don't have a marble slab or rolling pin, you may roll it out between sheets of cling film, lifting and replacing the cling film as the chocolate sheet stretches and grows. The chocolate should be no more than 3 mm/⅛ in thick.

4 Cut into shapes and press into place.

About keeping: Will keep for several months, wrapped and refrigerated.

Makes: Two 7.5 x 23 cm/3 x 9 in strips

USE FOR:
Chocolate Ribbon
Cake
Layered Custard
Cream Parfaits
Lightning Bolt
Dacquoise
Mango and
Chocolate Sorbets
Whiskey-Apricot
Chocolate Torte

EQUIPMENT:
Kitchen scales
Small bowl over
medium saucepan
Small spoon
Cling film
Marble slab
Rolling pin, marble
if possible
Scalpel; also variously
shaped biscuit cutter
and/or fluted
pastry wheel

44 *Caramelized Sugar Lattice*

USE FOR:
Layered Custard
 Cream Parfaits
Poached Pears
 with Gold Leaves

EQUIPMENT:
Kitchen scales
30 x 42.5 x 2.5/
 12 x 17 x 1 in Swiss
 roll tin or baking
 sheet
Baking parchment
Measuring spoons
Medium saucepan
Wooden spoon
Heatproof measuring
 jug

NOTES:

The dangerous reputation of the process of caramelizing sugar – the basis of so many wonderful confections, used here also in Pistachio Brittle on Chocolate (page 95) – can be daunting. Follow a few simple rules, however, and you will act with the assured finesse of an expert. Remember that the sugar is a molten mass that has gone beyond the boiling point and is therefore much hotter than the water that has boiled away. It is also very sticky. Avoid any skin contact; use only wooden implements that can't conduct the heat to your hand. Also, don't allow any foreign liquids to splash into the sugar at any time, or it may re-crystallize and could spit or boil over. Watch carefully and work quickly once the sugar is ready – when it cools it will be very hard and brittle. Clean utensils by soaking them overnight.

This decoration should not be attempted in very damp weather. The caramelized sugar will absorb the moisture from the air and re-liquefy.

INGREDIENTS:

Few drops vegetable oil
2 tablespoons water
100 g/3½ oz sugar

INSTRUCTIONS:

1 Smear the back of the Swiss roll tin or sheet with vegetable oil, then smooth a pan-size sheet of baking parchment on to it.

2 Pour the water carefully into a medium saucepan, sprinkle the sugar over and allow to absorb without stirring. Do not get any sugar on the sides of the pan.

3 Bring to the boil over medium heat – do not stir. Continue to boil, watching until all the water evaporates and sugar forms large, flat gooey crystals, then turns clear and syrupy before it begins to turn a golden colour towards the centre. Watch carefully as it colours, stirring with a wooden spoon to dissolve any remaining crystals.

When the sugar is golden brown, remove it from the heat. It's a good idea to set the tin on a metal, stone or ceramic-tile surface to conduct the intense heat away from the tin. This will slow down the cooking more quickly and help prevent the sugar from burning and getting bitter. Set aside for two minutes.

4 Pour the hot caramelized sugar into a dry heatproof measuring jug. (If you don't allow sugar to cool first, the denser shape the sugar assumes in the jug can raise the temperature sufficiently for it to boil out of the jug.) Begin to test the sugar's readiness by pouring a little in a corner of the tins. It should flow in a thin sticky, glossy stream rather than a sputtery splatter. When it reaches this point, cast a series of parallel lines by moving the stream back and forth across the tin, then cast another series in the opposite direction to form a lattice.

5 Allow to cool, then lift up the parchment paper and peel back to break into random shapes for decoration.

About keeping: If lattice bits are not to be used immediately, store in a dry, airtight container - and even by this method do not expect success in very damp weather.

Makes: One sheet sugar lattice

Index

ACKNOWLEDGEMENTS

This book is the result of the culinary collaboration and spiritual support of many friends and colleagues. I wish to thank: John Basgall for years of support and patient listening. John Baylin, who inspired me to write books, then inspired me to cook. Patricia Brabant, who had the confidence in me to begin this book six years ago ... a collaborator made in heaven. Carey Charlesworth, whose painstaking editing brought out the best in me. Edible Art of San Francisco, its founders Sharon Polster and Robin McMillian and present owner Meme Pederson, for providing the opportunities to do my very best. Tom Hart for encouragement and support. Greg Jeresek for his love and support. Laura Lamar for her selfless dedication to designing my fantasy in black and white. Donna Lazarus for her black and white squiggle plate. Amy Nathan, mentor and friend. David Rubenstein for his biscuit recipes and opinions. Christine Sansom and Preston Batt, who make sure I eat well when I can no longer bear to cook. Lucinda Young for her friendship, encouragement, support and selfless collaboration. Finally, my parents - who taught me what I wanted to know rather than what they expected me to learn.